Cybersecurity Jobs 3-in-1 Value Bundle:

Resume, Career Paths, and Work From Home

By

Bruce Brown, CISSP, ISC2 GRC

Download free ATS resume templates at:

convocourses.com/courses/resume

Check us out on:

youtube.com/convocourses

Contact us:

contact@convocourses.com

Table of Contents

Cryptographers / Mathematicians

Many people are familiar with mathematicians in academia, but mathematicians also work in many other fields, including:

Appendix A: DoD Approved Certifications

I love working from home!

Is WFH for you?

You can't always do Staycations

Working after hours

The Time Zone Differences

What You Need to have to Work From Home

Remote Work Restrictions

Types of Work from home Cybersecurity Jobs

Flex Work

Remote Work With Travel

Find a "Work from Home" Cybersecurity Job

Remote Work Resume

Work From Home Summary

Experience Working Remotely

Market Your WFH Resume

Find the Top 10 Job Sites

Create a Profile Post Your Resume

Apply for Remote Jobs

Use Alerts & Notifications

Be Open Minded

Avoid Scams

Work from home interview

The Screener

Hiring Manager and H.R. Department

Cybersecurity Jobs:

Resume Marketing

Book 1

Expected Results

I get nonstop job offers on my phone, via email and through direct messages. It actually gets annoying. But this is what you want ... options.

I receive offers with a variety of salaries, locations, and types of positions with all kinds of benefits and even short-term contracts that pay high but have no benefits. I have so many options that I am evaluating each employer and it's no big deal if I decide not to take that position or if they select someone else because I have so many other opportunities.

I have all these options because I know how to market a solid resume. I create searchable resumes for the jobs I am most qualified; then I post them on a lot of job sites.

These days all the tools that we need are there; we just need to know how to implement them.

To be honest, 90 percent of the jobs are not for me. There are a few reasons for this. It might be that the job is not even in my profession or it is in my profession but I'm not qualified for the position or sometimes I just don't want the position. I would say about 3 percent of the positions that are sent to me are something that would pay me well and I would be OK with the work.

I am OK with that 3 percent because the more I apply for, the better my chances of getting something I really want. And I could always settle for something in the 10 percent range. Those are usually the jobs with a long commute, or require me to move, or do some travel. Even the more uncomfortable options are a huge blessing. I am not worried during recessions, or if oil and gas prices are crazy.

No matter what, I am OK and my family is OK because I can find work or create work. That is the power of marketing yourself.

This book will walk you through how I have been able to get these kinds of results.

Obviously, everyone's results will vary. We all have different levels of experience, skill sets and qualifications, but by the end of this process you will have a method of opening more doors than ever before.

In this book we will focus mostly on cybersecurity jobs—but the techniques can be used in just about any profession, not just cybersecurity and information technology. If you are in health care, banking, retail, sanitation or any job that requires a resume, these methods can help you because ultimately, they are about marketing yourself effectively using your resume.

Steps to Take Action!

In order to have success and expanded opportunities, we need to go through the process of creating and positioning a resume that employers want. This book will help you create that resume.

We will use these steps:

- **Get tools** – There are basic things we need to have before we start.

- **ATS format** – In this section we go into detail about the application tracking software and the resume format that is necessary.

- **Work experience** – We will put the keywords together to show your cybersecurity experience and explore what is needed.

- **Degrees** – What degrees are needed for cybersecurity?

- **Certification** – Certain categories of cybersecurity prefer certain certifications.

- **Skills** – The skills section is a great opportunity to put in keywords.

- **Career paths** – Before we gather keywords, we need to know the direction you want to go with your career.

- **Find keywords** – This is research into what will be needed on your resume to make it more attractive.

- **Create a profile** – Before we market the resume, we need to create a profile.

- **Market the resume** – Where do you post your resume? How do you market yourself?

- **Appendix A:** entry-level certs – If you have little or no experience, you can check out these entry-level IT certifications to get an idea of where to start.

Tools You Will Need

There are some tools that will make this process much easier to do. In order to create our resume, we will start with software that can give us a blank page.

You can use a blank document on a word processor. Any of these will do:

- Microsoft Word
- Google Docs
- Open Office
- Apple Pages
- Notepad
- WordPad

Any of these will do. This document will not have any graphics, tables or fancy formatting.

The easiest thing to do is use one of my free templates at:

convocoures.com/courses/resume

We will be building your resume in a simple .doc or .docx in an arrangement that is acceptable to application tracking systems.

Set up marketing

How we set up marketing for the resume will depend on the industry you are trying to get into and the country you live in. This book focuses on cybersecurity and IT roles but the technique can work in just about any profession.

Let's start with countries. If you are in the United States or wanting to find a job in the USA, you will need accounts on the following sites:

- LinkedIn
- Dice.com
- Monster.com
- Ziprecruiter
- CareerBuilder
- Indeed.com
- Glassdoor
- AngelList
- PostJobFree
- Startupers
- Jobxoom
- Job Spider
- ReliefWeb
- Jobvertise

This list of job sites is ever changing so always do your own research. You just need the current list of top job sites in the country you want to work from.

Set up marketing for any country

No matter what country you are in or want to work from, you can market yourself there. There is no guarantee that you can get work there, but it doesn't hurt to try.

Each country has a different set of job sites that works better there so we need to find that top 10. To find them, go to your favorite search engine and type: "Top 10 job sites [country]."

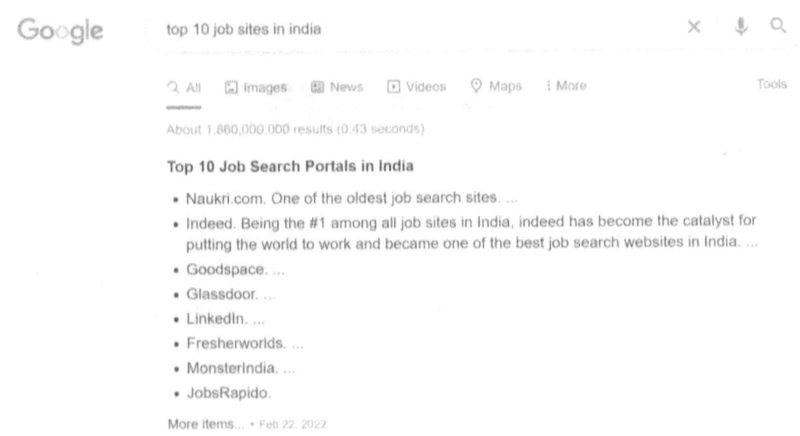

In this case we searched for "Top 10 job sites in India." Our results as of this writing are the following:

- Naukri.com

- Indeed

- Goodspace

- Glassdoor

- LinkedIn

- Fresherworlds

- MonsterIndia

- JobsRapido

- Upwork

- Shine

A few pointers about this search. Avoid the paid ad links. Go to the top organic results. Also, compare your list against at least two other top lists. You will find job sites that pop up among the top of the same lists. These are your first priority.

Another alternative is to look for remote jobs in multiple countries and work from whatever country you want.

What Is ATS?

The resume we will build will be arranged to be acceptable to application tracking systems (ATS). An ATS is software that most recruiters and employers use to track candidates as they go through the recruiting process.

An ATS-style resume is very simple with sections labeled a certain way, with no fancy-looking formats or fonts. The sections and labels we will address in separate chapters. The recommended fonts are Times New Roman, Calibri, Arial, or Georgia.

Organizations (corporate or government) ATS systems can be built into a database that allows them to collect and sort through hundreds of resumes they have collected or it can be a full suite of tools that make it possible to analyze all potential candidates.

An application tracking system helps the organization do the following:

Make the onboarding process faster

With a specific format that has all of the data they need from each candidate, the employer can make sure they have everything they need to start work.

Be competitive

Most of the top 500 largest companies in the United States (Fortune 500 companies) use an ATS system because it makes the hiring process easier. Each of these companies is competing to get the best and brightest hired as quicky as possible before their competition gets them.

9

More efficient and cheaper

With a streamlined method of collecting information from potential candidates, the organization can give fewer tasks to their recruiters. This tool helps them sort through more resumes faster.

Find qualified candidates faster

With standardized data collected from the ATS resume, the organization can use artificial intelligence and machine learning to identify skills and predict success factors that help them find the best fit.

The bottom line is that the ATS resume makes it easier for the employer to find you and hire you.

How ATS works

The application tracking system processes each resume by breaking it into sections. These sections are important to cybersecurity:

- Work Experience
- Education
- Skills
- Languages
- Certifications

There are other sections that ATS can read but these are the most essential that we will stick to in this book.

ATS searches for keywords, key phrases and qualifications to see if your resume matches the job description.

Here is an example of how ATS sees your cybersecurity resume:

"Motivated expert with 3 years of experience in cybersecurity. Extensive troubleshooting on TCP/IP networking issues. Proven track record of success, employer satisfaction, and strong communication skills. Security clearance: secret."

ATS sees:

"Cybersecurity"

"3 years of experience"

"TCP/IP"

"Networking"

"Strong communication skills"

"Security clearance"

Then, ATS matches what it gathers from your resume to the organizations list of requirements:

Cybersecurity [CHECK]

3 years of experience [CHECK]

TCP/IP [CHECK]

Communication skills [CHECK]

CCNA [missing]

Microsoft Office [missing]

This is just an example of things that might be checked based on the ATS assessing your resume keywords, key phrases and qualifications against a job's requirements. If your resume doesn't match the requirements, ATS will rate your resume accordingly and move on to the next.

Avoid the following items on your resume:

- Text boxes
- Logos
- Images
- Headers/footers
- Tables
- Hyperlinks

- Uncommon fonts (stick with Cambria, Times New Roman, Georgia, Arial, Helvetica, Garamond)

Popular ATS systems

If you have ever uploaded your resume or filled out an online job application in the past 5 years, there is a good chance you have used one of the more popular ATS systems. These include:

Taleo by Oracle. This system goes back to the 1990s. This system owns something like 20 percent of the market share for ATS systems and 30 percent of the Fortune 500. Corporations like Starbucks, Nike, Deloitte and Tesla have used Taleo.

iCIMS. I see iCIMS a lot on government contracting companies. It has about 7 percent of the ATS market share and has been used by Amazon, Samsung and Uber. Candidates are sorted based on the percentage of keyword matches and the same keyword can be used multiple times.

Greenhouse. This ATS is being used by Major League Baseball, Roku and Taco Bell. They go by keyword frequency. At the time of this writing, they have about 8 percent of the ATS market.

Other ATS systems you may have heard of include Jobvite, BrassRing, Workday, SAP, CareerBuilder and there are many others. About 8 percent of companies have their own proprietary ATS system.

What they all have in common is their focus on the sections and keywords to match job requirements. So, what you need to know is what job you are targeting (career path), what keywords to put in for that target job and what sections you need on your ATS resume. There are the things we will focus on in this book.

ATS Resume Format and Sections

The first thing you will notice about the ATS-style resume is that it is simple. It does not have fancy graphic overlays or comprehensive tables that break down all the skills and certifications. In fact, these things disrupt the ATS system so we must avoid this at all costs. The final files will be a .doc, .docx or .txt. We can also make it a PDF, but some older ATS systems cannot process PDFs so I would avoid this.

Bruce Brown

Email: contact@convocourses.com | **Phone:** (719) 470-0703 | **Address:** Colorado, CO 80017 | **Linkedin:** linkedin.com/in/bruce-cissp-rmf

Summary

Remote work preferred. I have a CISSP, with 20 years of experience doing cybersecurity. I have done many roles including Information System Security Officer (ISSO), Cybersecurity analysis and consulting. My specialty is NIST Risk Management Framework (RMF) and other security frameworks.

Work Experience

Cyber Risk Programs Security Consultant II

Verizon / Remote, Colorado / 09/2019 – 05/2022
- Mapped security controls and policy to NIST 800-53, NIST CSF, CIS controls and ISO 27001 frameworks; mapped 100s of controls for 2 clients to determine compliance with 3 -4 frameworks.
- Cyber Threat Intelligence (CTI) analyst work using open-source and commercial intelligence tools to identify communicate, and mitigate cyber threats before they can impact clients. Found over 100 leaked credentials. Took organizations from having multiple breaches to reducing risks and earning an interim authority to operate within 200 days.
- Conducted PCI-DSS assessment on multiple sites around the world; resulting in 3 compliant PCI-DSS networks with over 100 systems.
- Created training for cybersecurity team's security assessment report (SAR) review process improving the cyber security risk assessment process for all 20 people on the team.
- Implemented general attack strategies such as MITRE ATT&CK framework that help

Basic ATS Resume

We need to have simple headers. Do not get creative with the headers in the resume.

Instead of saying something like "Where I have worked" as a header, we will keep it to "Work Experience." Instead of "My Skills," we will just say "Skills." For the sake of the ATS that the resume will get plugged into, we need to keep it plain and take the guesswork out of the equation. ATS knows what "Skills" means; however, it might not be able to parse "MY SKILLS" or "Professional Skills."

We will show the best format for each section of the ATS resume.

Your resume should be focused on one role and get straight to the point. For example, if you are trying to get a role in management, network administration or cloud computing then you need a resume that focuses on each one of these. The management resume should focus on your management skills and experience; your cloud computing should focus on cloud certifications, cloud skills and cloud experience. And the same goes for the network administration role.

If I go all the way back to the beginning of my career, I was actually a security guard in the air force. I won't include this on my resume for a security operations center (SOC) analyst position because the skills set for a SOC analyst has almost nothing to do with the skills I required as a security guard. But I might include the security guard experience on my resume to get a security control assessor (SCA) role because some SCAs conduct physical assessments just like security guards do. There is actual overlap in the experience skill sets and even certifications.

Mention your personal details & contact information

The resume should start with your name and contact information.

Bruce Brown

Email: contact@convocourses.com | **Phone:** (719) 470-0703 | **Address:** Colorado, CO 80017 | **Linkedin:** linkedin.com/in/bruce-cissp-rmf

Now, what you have to remember is that your name and contact information will be publicly available. What I do is use an alias. I use my middle name and a different last name. It's too easy for someone to use my real name and figure out things I don't want them to know.

For more details on protecting your privacy, see the chapter on profiles.

Example of an ATS-friendly resume

Here is an example of a cybersecurity resume with the ATS template:

Brian Noble

Summary

IT & cybersecurity specialist with a secret security clearance eligibility and 2 years of experience in IT & cybersecurity at a medium-sized company. Well-developed skills implementing security controls and ensuring that servers and end-user devices (Windows and MAC) are configured securely.

506-124-6898 – BriNobes554@outlook.com – Fayetteville, North Carolina, 28303

Education

Associate Degree – Information Technology – Fayetteville Community College – 2019

- Working on BS in CS
- Extensive training using digital spreadsheets and formulas efficiently
- Earned a certificate in Security+ lab

Certifications

CompTIA Security + Certification

Project Management Professional Certification (PMP)

Work Experience

Help Desk Support – TirePlanet – April 2021–April 2022

- Troubleshooting end-users' laptops with network and software issues; support 150 users with multiple devices

- Managed Android and iPhone ensuring all company-owned mobile devices are tracked and data is encrypted
- Enabled audit logs on 34 mission-essential systems and 100 end-user laptops to conduct continuous monitoring and detect possible security incidents
- Created an incident response plan for all business essential servers supporting the southwest sites; virtual servers include Windows 2019 and RedHat systems

IT Customer Service – Ants – New Mexico – January 2020–December 2021

- Conducted quarterly risk assessment on over 200 business critical systems; created risk reports for the CIO and upper management
- Assisted the server team in installing 12 Windows 2019 servers migrating legacy systems to a new operating system
- Provided remote technical support for the workstations of over 1,500 customers; patient with difficult customers

Skills

- Programming language: C+, HTML, Fortran, COBOL
- Security clearance: Secret, TS/SCI, Public Trust

We will go into each section of the cybersecurity ATS resume so that we can increase the chances of getting more opportunities in this lucrative career path.

Summary Section

Label this section as "Summary" or "Objectives." I use "Summary" because it is more flexible. An Objective is a goal or thing aimed at, but a summary can be an introduction to your best skills and it can include goals if you want.

This section is a great opportunity to put in more keywords, explain what you are looking for and mentions your security clearance (if you have one). From what I have seen, ATS systems don't have a section for summary, but it does recognize it and pull out keywords that might relate to the job requirements. For this reason, we want to add our most powerful and impactful keywords and qualifications in the summary to slap the technical recruiter right in the face!

The email and contact information can come before, after or even be put into the summary. The ATS system will find your contact information, but for the sake of the human who will eventually review the resume, I usually label the Summary and keep the contacts up top just under my name.

For samples of ATS-style resumes check out:

convocourses.com/courses/resume

Here is what I put in one of my most recent summaries:

Summary:

> Prefer remote work. Twenty years of experience in cybersecurity implementing NIST 800 RMF with the public and private sector including interacting with federal government agencies such as the Department of Defense and NASA. Public Trust Level 6; DoD Secret security clearance (inactive), TS

(inactive). Working on my AWS Certified Cloud Practitioner certification.

And a more effective way to list the summary would be to bulletize it. This will allow the humans who have to read it to absorb the information faster.

Summary:

- Prefer remote work
- 20 years of experience in cybersecurity
- NIST 800 RMF with the public and private sector
- Experience with federal government agencies such as the Department of Defense and NASA
- Public Trust Level 6; DoD Secret security clearance (inactive), TS (inactive)
- Working on my AWS Certified Cloud Practitioner certification

I put all the things that have the most impact and were the most important to me personally.

1. **Remote work.** I am telling them right away what I prefer. At the time, it was very important that I get remote work.
2. **Experience level.** I put all my years of experience. This is my most hard-hitting statement, because I know how important it is for the positions I am seeking.
3. **Keywords:** Keywords and phrases include "information system security," "NIST 800," "RMF," "Department of Defense," "DoD," "NASA." I know that ATS systems will pick up on these keywords.
4. **Security clearance:** Security clearance should have its own section, but since it doesn't, and I know it's something that some organizations look for, I put it right up top in the summary.
5. **Sneaky tactic:** The last sentence I put in is "working on" my AWS cloud certification. At the time of this writing, I don't have this certification. But by mentioning that I am working on it, I

have now listed this keyword on my resume. I know that cloud technology is hot in my industry so I wanted to get it in there.

The summary should have your biggest strengths and best keywords condensed into how you can help the organization. You can use this same verbiage for your online profiles, which we will talk about later.

Keep the summary down to a few sentences. Don't write a novel. Get to the point. This section is optional, but you really want to use it to put in more keywords, sneak in your most hard-hitting assets, and your security clearance (if you have one).

Work Experience Section

List this section of your resume as "Work Experience" or "Experience." This is potentially the most important part of your resume and has the potential to get you a cybersecurity job the fastest because you list the most keywords, actions and impacts on the organization. This tells the story of your skills and what you can bring to the table.

Here is an example of an ATS-style work experience listed on a resume:

Work Experience

Verizon, Cybersecurity Analyst II, Herndon, VA – 09/2019 – 05/2022

- Performed cyber threat analysis using tools like Recorded Future for a private company whose assets were under attack by external threat actors; took the organization from having multiple breaches to having a low risk and earning a full security certification within a year.

For this section, ATS systems are looking for six things on your resume:

- Label "Work Experience" or "Experience"
- Work role
- Company you worked at
- Dates range you worked
- Location
- Bullets with keywords

We will go much deeper into what needs to go into this section of the resume when we dive into "Keywords in Work Experience".

Education Section

You need to put your highest level of relevant education on your resume. This means if you are looking for an entry-level position, that will require a GED or a high school diploma. If the job requires a bachelor's or master's degree or PhD, you will need to put this on your resume in the "Education" section.

The education section on an ATS format resume needs to have the following:

- Name of institution
- Degree
- School location
- Years attended

First, list the section as "Education." Then add the degree followed by the college, the location and year of graduation.

Here is the ATS format for the "Education" section of your resume:

Education

Associate Degree – Information Systems – Missouri University School of Business – 2017

- Completed an online course in cloud technology
- Extensive training using network scanners
- Earned a certificate in blockchain technology

*The extra bullets allow you to add more keywords. Here are more good examples of cybersecurity degrees listed.

- *Bachelor of Applied Sciences (B.A.Sc.), International Business, 2012, Illinois State University, Bloomington, IL*

- *George Washington University, 2000–2004*
  Bachelor of Arts, Information Technology

- *Bachelor of Engineering, Electrical Engineering, 2008*
  Vanderbilt University, Nashville, TN

- *University of Rome, Italy, Bachelor's Degree, Applied*
  Mathematics, 2001

Even if you didn't get your degree but finished some college, you can still list what you did. It's still acceptable to include your college education if it's relevant to the job requirements. What you will do is list the number of credits obtained. For example:

University of Phoenix, Santa Fe, AZ

Computer Science, 55 Credit Hours Obtained

While we are on the topic of degrees, you should know that there are cybersecurity jobs that don't require a degree. Some entry-level positions are more focused on someone willing to get in and do the work.

Most high-paying cybersecurity jobs will require a degree. If you have some combination of high-level security clearance, specific experience or skills the organization needs or an IT certification that they require, then sometimes organizations will overlook the lack of a degree for these high-paying positions.

Acceptable degrees in cybersecurity

There is a misconception about the required degrees in cybersecurity roles. Many people think that you must have a degree specifically in cybersecurity to get a cybersecurity role. While there are positions that call for a very specific degree in cybersecurity, most will take any computer-related degree. This includes information technology, information system, information management, database, computer science, data analytics or any other degree with a direct connection to computers.

In fact, with some experience or technical skills in computers or if you can prove that you can do the work, many cybersecurity roles will take any science, technical, engineering, or mathematics (STEM) degree.

If all of this is discouraging you because you don't have a degree, or you have a degree in liberal arts, don't be discouraged about getting into cybersecurity. I have known a few cybersecurity badasses making crazy money with no degree. Two of my technical mentors (among the most gifted people whom I have ever met to this day) did not have a degree. And they would talk really bad about anyone who said they had one. My argument to them was that these days many companies are asking for an academic qualification and it's easier to find a good job if you have one.

One of my former coworkers had a master's degree in Egyptology (which I didn't even know was a thing). He worked with me doing NIST 800 security compliance. And another coworker could sing really well; turns out his degree was music or something. He was one of the smartest guys on the team. What all of these people had in common was that they had something that the organization wanted. Some skill. Some experience. Some certification.

Certifications Section

If you have IT certifications you should list them on your resume. Do not add expired or irrelevant certifications. For example, the CompTIA Security+ actually needs to be maintained with annual fees and continuing education. If these are not met, then the certification will expire. Once expired, don't add it to your resume. These certifications are very easy for employers to check so don't lie about it.

Do not add irrelevant certifications on your resume that is focused on a specific cybersecurity role. For example, if you are going for a cybersecurity analyst position at a security operation center (SOC) at a government agency, you should not add your certified nursing assistant certifications on the resume. But if you are going for an information manager job at a hospital, adding all of your health-care-related certifications and licenses will help you.

Here are how certifications should be added.

Certifications

CompTIA Security + Certification

Project Management Professional Certification (PMP)

List out the full name of the certification and if there is an acronym, add that as well. This does two things. It allows an application tracking system to pull the information provided into its database and match it to the known certifications that it has stored and it adds two keywords for job search engines.

In my experience, the hierarchy of resume highlights are experience, computer or STEM degree, and IT certifications related to the role. I have seen more people with experience and a certification get jobs than I have people with just a degree and no experience get a job. And in cybersecurity, even if they get in with no experience and a master's degree, their pay might suffer. Experience holds a lot of weight.

But don't sleep on certifications. Depending on the cert, it can be like steroids for your salary when you put it on your resume. The ISC2 CISSP, Certified Information Systems Security Professional, changed my life.

I am offered way more money; employers are constantly contacting me. I am asked to teach lower security certifications. And sometimes, employers don't even care if I have a degree because they see the CISSP and the skills they want.

But CISSP is not even the best cybersecurity certification!

The best certification is the one that most employers in your career path are asking for. That could be a Certified Ethical Hacker (CEH), CompTIA Security+, SANS GIAC Intrusion Analyst certification (GCIA) or any number of IT certs. It really depends on whatever the organization has a requirement for. And with the research you are going to do on keywords for your chosen career path, you will know what IT certifications are needed.

Check cybersecurity category certifications

Each category of cybersecurity has a specific set of certifications that are required or preferred or just helpful to landing roles within the specialty areas. Categories are described in the chapter on career paths and in much greater detail in book 2 of this series as well as the National Initiative for Cybersecurity Careers and Study (niccs.cisa.gov).

I am in the category of Oversee and Govern under the specialty area of Information System Security Manager (ISSM). In my experience, the top certifications are some of the following:

- CISSP
- CASP
- CISM

- CISA
- ISC2 CAP
- Security+

Penetration tester and ethical hackers are in the cybersecurity category of Oversee and Govern as well as Analyze. They have the specialty area of Network Services and Exploitation analysis. These specialty areas include certain certifications that hold more weight. Some of these certifications include (but are not limited to):

- OSCP
- GPEN
- CEH

Each category of cybersecurity has its own group of certifications that employers look for. Even if you don't have the preferred certifications, you can put on your resume that you are "Working on the CEH." You can put this in the summary of the resume so that anyone looking for a CEH, will see your resume pop up.

We will go into certifications, cybersecurity career paths and cybersecurity categories in greater detail in book 2. See appendix A for recommended entry-level certifications.

Skills Section

The "Skills" part of the resume is an excellent opportunity to add more keywords. This section is a great way to show skills that you did not put in the summary or work experience section. The skills section allows you to get straight to the point rather than trying to list every keyword in the experience section.

One thing to remember is that you are not just stuffing keywords here. If you cannot explain how you used the skill during a possible interview, then you should not list it. Consider this: if it is a skill they really need at their organization, they will ask you about it.

One time I mentioned "cloud" on my resume. At the time, my only experience with cloud was that I'd gotten a cloud-based system certified a few times. I did not have experience implementing or maintaining a cloud-based system. But since I mentioned it on my resume, the manager asked me about every aspect of cloud and cloud security for 15 minutes straight. He went from a complex technical question about Microsoft Azure versus Amazon AWS implementations to examining risks of cloud scans. And when I could not answer any of those questions, he asked general questions on the differences between PaaS versus SaaS. Finally, he gave up and said, "OK, you know what ... we will avoid the cloud-based questions. I don't want to waste your time or mine."

He said this because I could not answer many of those questions. I was saying things like, "Sir, I am not sure about that one. I have never actually implemented Azure or AWS." Or "I am not going to try to BS my way through that technical question. I don't know the answer." Or "My only experience with cloud was getting them an authorization to operate. I am familiar with the FedRAMP process, which focuses on cloud compliance."

This entire line of questioning was based on me mentioning cloud twice. My point is that you should only list skills that you can speak on in some way. Because if the organization really needs that skill, they will definitely ask about it.

How to list skills

You can list skills at the bottom or top of the resume. But I list them at the bottom of the resume. I do this because, the summary is where I need to put my best assets. Next, I usually put either work experience or education because education is short and work experience is a better way to sell your skills, in my opinion.

When I do this section, I focus on the most relevant hard skills for the job I am targeting in cybersecurity.

Here is a great way to group your skills together:

> **Skills**
>
> Programming: C+, HTML, Fortran, COBOL, ADA
>
> Security Compliance: PCI/DSS, NIST 800, NIST CSF, SOX, HIPAA
>
> Security Analysis: Network forensics, Tcpdump, Wireshark fundamentals, silk, traffic analysis tools, intrusion detection system, packet engineering
>
> Network Engineering: Cisco configuration, Cisco backups, IOS troubleshooting, RIP, OSPF, NAT, DHCP configuration

In this example we are making it easy for recruiters to read, and for an ATS system to accept. We are grouping similar skills together. We are also using skills relevant to the job we are trying to get. If you want to target another job, you can create a separate resume and add different keywords that are relevant to that job.

You can categorize the skills by types of technology, levels of proficiency or even vendors. The most important thing is that they are relevant to the career you are interested in.

Here are more examples:

Skills

System Administration: Active Directory, SCCM management, account management

Security Control Implementation: manage event log, manage audit logs, MS Windows hardening, configuration management, change control, disaster recovery plan

Cybersecurity tools: Nessus scanner, Wireshark, Nmap expert, Qualys, network scan, vulnerability manager

Skills

Programming

C+

HTML

Fortran

COBOL

ADA

Security Compliance

PCI/DSS

Security clearance tip:

If you have a security clearance, the skills section is a great place to add it. The security clearance does not have its own section so we have to list it where we can. Make sure you put it on top in the summary, but here is an example of how you could list it in skills as well.

Skills:

Programming language: C+, HTML, Fortran, COBOL

Security clearance: Secret, TS/SCI, Public Trust

Choose a Career Path

Now that we know the proper format of the cybersecurity ATS resume we need to choose the keywords to put into our resume. But before we can drill down on the keywords for the resume, we need to know what career path to choose.

You can choose a career path, but sometimes a career path chooses you! What I mean is you may already be in a career. Maybe it is a career you don't like, or something you are bored with, or perhaps you don't even know that you are in a career. You will know your current career path based on where most of your experience is. You may be able to use your current career as leverage to get into a path you want. Even if you are a sanitation engineer and want to be in cybersecurity, there may be a way to use the current organization you are in to start doing IT, which will lead to cybersecurity, or (at the very least) you can use the income from your job to invest in your education in IT and cybersecurity.

From IT to cybersecurity

If you are already working in information technology, you probably already have cybersecurity experience. You just need to add all of the security-related experience to your resume. We will go through some of the things that you can put on your resume to reflect your cybersecurity experience in the "Keywords in Work Experience" chapter. But first you need to know about the different specializations and categories in cybersecurity.

Cyber Security Workforce categories

National Initiative for Cybersecurity Careers and Studies (NICCS) has a comprehensive breakdown of cybersecurity categories, specialty areas and work roles in the cybersecurity workforce. Their categorization is a good way to understand which direction you want to go in with IT and cybersecurity.

Categories include:

- **Securely Provision** – architect and design secure information systems. The specializations in this category are:
  - Risk management
  - Software development
  - System architecture
  - System development
  - Systems requirements planning
  - Technology R&D
  - Test & evaluation
- **Oversee and Govern** – manage and guide so the organization can effectively conduct cybersecurity. The Specialty Areas include:
  - Cybersecurity management
  - Executive cyber leadership
  - Legal advice
  - Program / project management and acquisition
  - Strategic planning and policy
  - Training
- **Protect and Detect** – identify, analyze threats to internal information systems and networks. There are only a few Specialty Areas in this category:
  - Cyber defense analysis
  - Cyber defense infrastructure support
  - Incident response
  - Vulnerability assessment and management

- **Collect and Operate** – gather cybersecurity information that may be used to develop intelligence. Collect and Operate has these specialties:
    - Collection operations
    - Cyber operational planning
    - Cyber operations
- **Investigate** – investigate security events or crimes related to information technology. Investigate has two Specialty Areas:
    - Cyber investigation (cybersecurity analyst)
    - Forensics
- **Operate and Maintain** – provide support, administration and maintenance to ensure effective and efficient information systems performance and security. Here are the specialties:
    - Customer services / technical support
    - Data admin
    - Network services
    - System admin
- **Analyze** – review and evaluate incoming cybersecurity information to determine its usefulness for intelligence. Analyze has the following Specialty Areas:
    - Exploit analysis
    - Threat analysis
    - Targets
    - All-source analysis

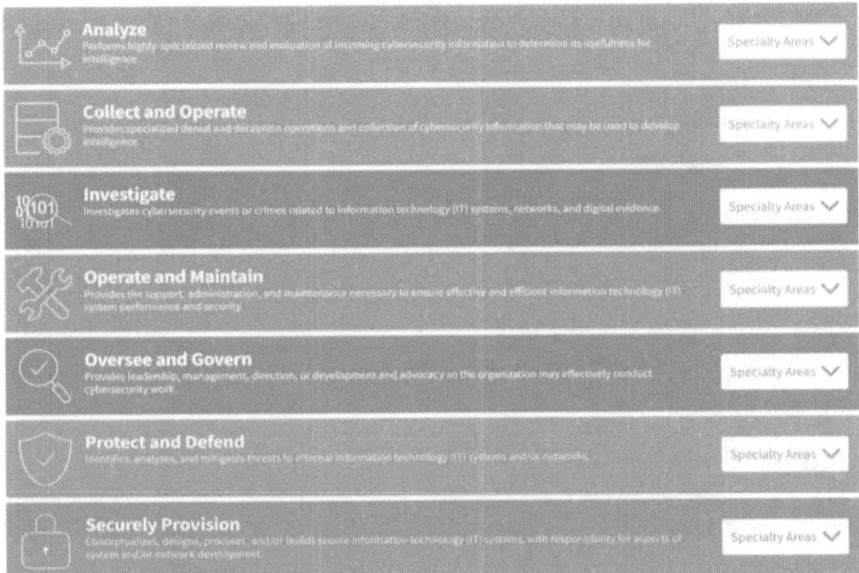

These cybersecurity workforce categories and specialty areas will be covered more in-depth in book 2 of this series. For now, what we need to know is that cybersecurity includes management, policy, administrative technical, analytical and many other types of positions. The main takeaway is that cybersecurity is very diverse and requires many different types of experience, knowledge and skills. It's not just hacking.

The popular cybersecurity skill sets of hacking, coding and cracking have been popularized in movies, television and social media but as you can see there are seven categories with dozens of specialized areas and hundreds of roles to perform these cybersecurity jobs.

In my experience, most of the work roles in the Oversee and Govern category do not require any hands-on technical skills. There are some categories dedicated to analysis with nothing but analytical jobs. The investigation category is where you find digital forensics (another popular cybersecurity area).

In order to figure out which category to pursue, look at three factors:

- Interest
- Skills
- Money

Interests

Your interest in the cybersecurity category is important because it will determine if you will stick with what you may need to learn and how quickly you pick up the skills necessary. Interests can also make the job you choose fun.

Skills

With the right skills you can get into the position you want more easily. If you have the skills, you need to put them on your resume with keywords. If you don't have the skills, you need to identify what skills, tools and experience you need to acquire so you can put them on your resume.

Money

Last but not least, "Show me the money!" You should consider the money. If the IT or cybersecurity category seems like a good fit but the money is not quite there, you need to think about the time and resources you are going to put in and whether or not it is worth your time. Now, you have to understand that most entry-level positions are not going to start off with a great income, so when you consider the money, think about the end goal. If the work roles that you are building toward will not end up close to the kind of income you want, you may need to consider something else.

From cook to IT professional services

He was five years into his career as a chef when he realized that most of them don't make much money.

They say, "follow your dreams" or "if you do what you love you never have to work again" or "follow your passion." Frank Johnson did this but he found out the hard way that his "passion" was not quite paying his bills.

He had a degree from the Cambridge School of Culinary Arts. He managed to earn a position as a chef in two of the top restaurants in Boston within three years. But his dream was to make his own menu, create his own meals.

The first time he'd done so was for his mother when he was 12 years old. He brought her a hot bowl of minestrone, with clams, dried cannellini, white wine, lima beans and some of his own special ingredients. He remembers the smile on her face when she asked him, "Franky, did you make this?"

That's when he knew he had a talent for taste. He was spectacular with the spoon.

He'd won third place in the Concord Chili Cook-Off at 16 years old and he had won his wife's heart with recipe he'd concocted from his soul. He had validation of his skills and he knew he wanted to share this talent with the world.

Against his father's advice, he'd enrolled in the school of culinary arts. At his first job at one of the top ten restaurants in Massachusetts, he realized almost immediately that being a chef felt more like a job than art. He wasn't creating and being innovative; he was memorizing recipes of someone else's dreams and creativity.

He knew what was missing. He knew what he had to do. But he needed a little help.

"Dad, hear me out." Frank put a hand on his old man's shoulders and gave him that sly handsome grin that he'd inherited. For a moment it was like looking into a future mirror. His old man was just an aged reflection of himself. "I know how you feel about my work and—"

"You mean cooking." Pops shook his head. "How's the pay? Is it as good as engineering?"

Frank nodded. "I know you wanted me to be an engineer like you. But—"

"Franky," his pop said, laughing, "you know you're like your mother. So stubborn. Son, just tell me how much you need."

"Dad, it's not like that. I wanted to tell you that you were right. Just hear me out." Frank squeezed his father's broad shoulders.

Frank Senior sighed. "I'm listening."

Frank looked out into a dream and used his hand to present an imaginary sign: "Franky's Italian Bistro."

His dad shook his head and nodded. "You want to start a restaurant?"

"Not just any restaurant, Dad." Frank smiled. "'Our' restaurant. A family restaurant."

Frank Senior was silent. He wanted to tell his son that being a chef and being a business owner were not the same thing. He wanted to break down the statistics of what happens to most businesses within 3 years and tell him about his own business that failed.

But instead, being a positive and encouraging parent, he signed a check.

Almost immediately, Frank junior realized that the restaurant business was not for him. He had to secure property, deal with banks, set up point-of-sale devices, choose designs and furniture, hire people. These things took him away from his passion. In fact, he eventually had to hire another person to be the chef!

Three years later, Frank Johnson was closing up the restaurant and enrolling in something he didn't particularly love but happened to be good at. Engineering. Software engineering, to be exact. He had a job at an IT company fixing computers before he even finished his degree in computer science. He made more in the first two years as a computer engineer than he did in five years of being a chef.

Frank still cooks, but he does it for his family.

I knew the actual cook who became an engineer

This is based on a true story. When I was working as a contractor for the army in the Middle East, we had to build a security information event manager (SIEM) from scratch on three different networks. The army had an agreement with the SIEM vendor. We needed their help on the first install and training on their product.

They sent three very sharp guys from professional services. I worked with them for about a week. We were on our way to lunch when I said to the team leader, "You're really good at this. You're writing scripts, setting up networks, configuring the system. How did you get into this?"

He smiled and said, "This wasn't my first choice. This is just a job for me. I was a chef for about five years."

I was shocked. That's when he told me about how being a chef made barely enough money to live.

"We cannot all be Anthony Bourdain or Gordon Ramsey, you know!" He laughed.

I could relate to this. Cybersecurity was not my first choice. I wanted to be a writer. My English teachers would often read what I wrote in front of the class. And this happened all the way to college. One of my teachers had a talent scout from Stanford interview me and check out my work when I was in high school. I submitted a dozen short stories to fiction magazines I read and got back-to-back rejection letters.

Looking back, I think there was nothing stopping me from continuing to write and try different genres, but by the time I became an adult I realized how much harder being a writer or an artist was than doing something like engineering. Besides, I was obsessed with computers.

I am not telling you to abandon your dreams. But what I learned was that it is a strategic move to get a job that makes good money to support your artistic goals and fantastic dreams.

After all, Frank didn't really cook for money as much as he just loved the joy it gave people to taste his delicious creations. And for me, writing is like a spiritual exercise. Making money with things I write is icing on the cake. Currently, I give too much of my content out for free to make a livable wage from it, so I have a job and writing is a hobby/side hustle until something goes viral. Hey, it could happen!

What to choose

Go through the categories listed. You can also do a search for "NICE Cyber Workforce" and check out the complete breakdown of all the special areas and job titles under each category. In book 2 of this series, we will deep dive into each Cybersecurity Workforce category and the requirements of each.

Choose something that makes a decent wage, something within your capacity to do and something you are comfortable with. For example, I did IT field support long enough to realize it did not make the kind of money I needed to support my lifestyle. I know my math skills are not good enough to do something like cryptography. And I am not yet comfortable as a manager. The jobs I have tried that worked for me are cybersecurity analysis, information system security officer and information system security engineering.

I have tried network engineering, customer support, programming and other positions that were really not for me, but helped to expand my knowledge and experience.

Tips for choosing the right career:

- Study the requirements necessary for a career
- Study the salary range of a career
- Study the industry of the career
- Try different jobs in a career path
- Talk to people already in the career path you want

Requirements of a career

Each career path has certain requirements at certain levels and categories within. If you become a help desk professional in the category of "Operate and Maintain" in the cyber workforce, one of the requirements will be the skill of troubleshooting workstations. The organization may have additional requirements such as certain IT certifications. In the role of a chief information officer, in the category of "Oversee and Govern," the requirement is different. The requirement might include 10 years of experience in a management role, a management degree and a background investigation.

Study the requirements of a career by looking at jobs in that career. Pay attention to the job descriptions, requirements and job preferences.

Salary range

Use search engines to see what the salary range of a career is. Look up job titles in the career path you are looking into. There are some pretty good sites that are out at the time of this writing. These include:

- Glassdoor
- Salary.com
- PayScale

Pay close attention to the average. The low and high parts of the pay are heavily affected by the locations, years of experience and the quality of the company. Some companies pay all their employees much higher than average companies. Facebook, Google, Apple, and

Microsoft, for example, pay way higher. Another factor of pay to consider is the cost of living of the employees. Some organizations will pay you based on the cost of living of where you reside. Other factors that affect salary are security clearance and the level of responsibility. If the organization requires security clearances, sometimes they will pay a little higher than normal. Management, director or C-level positions will usually pay higher because there is more responsibility, stress, hours and pressure in those positions.

Study the industry

In the case of forensics in the "Investigation" category, studying the industry surrounding forensics will give you an idea of what is expected, who is hiring, what organizations have a need for forensics, and the types of people who get into this field. Watching videos from people in the industry you want to get into is very helpful. Pay NO attention to TV shows and movies that give a false impression of the job. If you watched the movie *Hackers* you would think that hacking was flying through a 1990s 3D rendering of "cyberspace." If you watched the movie *Swordfish*, you would think that all hackers look like Storm and Wolverine.

Hackers look more like Napoleon and Pedro.

If you want to see a realistic hacker movie, check out *The Girl with the Dragon Tattoo*, *War Games* and for TV shows check out *Mr. Robot* ...

Listen to people in the career path

One of the best ways to know whether or not any career path is for you is to listen to the good, the bad and ugly about the jobs in that space. If you want to be a pediatrician, listen to people who have been doing it for years. Listen to the men and women who love it and those who recently quit the profession. Listen to the horror stories of pediatricians. If you still want the career after that, then you are ready.

Use your job as leverage for the new career

If you are in a job right now and hope to expand into something else, you can use that job to get something you like. If you are getting paid, fund your path to another career. Fund your education by buying books and courses that teach you the skills and knowledge you need to start your new job. Pay for a degree, certification or license in the new field. This will take some work on your part, but if you really want the new path, you must stick with it.

Careers that can get you into IT

You can really go from any career field and transition into information technology if you want. I was a security guard in the air force and I cross-trained into computers. There are some career fields that are hungry for information technology professionals and cybersecurity people. Here are a few of them:

- Health care
- Law
- Financial sector
- Intelligence
- Government
- Critical infrastructures (pipeline, oil, gas, electric)

There are certain aspects of these career fields that might allow you to make a lateral move into IT or cybersecurity.

Health care – Health-care professionals have terminology and industry standards that most workers in this field have to know. For example, Health Insurance Portability and Accountability Act of 1996 (HIPAA) compliance and protection of patient information. There are actual IT professions that only exist in health care. Being a nurse, a Certified Nursing Assistant (CAN) or any other health-care professional can help you get a job in this field as an IT or cybersecurity professional at a medical institute if you get to know the basics of IT.

Law – When I transitioned from law enforcement to cybersecurity, I was surprised that there were many concepts that were relevant to both fields. For one thing the concepts of access control, assessments, privacy and logs are used extensively in law, law enforcement and security. As evidence has become more digitized, it has become more important to protect it as it goes through the legal system. Concepts like "chain of custody" make immediate sense to some in cybersecurity, particularly digital forensics. Forensics investigators are a part of law enforcement and investigations. It is also part of cybersecurity. If you are in law, physical security, investigations or the criminal justice system, you may be able to make a lateral change into IT or cybersecurity.

Financial sector – If you are in banking, investing, tax law, or funds management then you should know there is a big need for cybersecurity personnel who have some understanding of the financial sector. Deloitte, Ernst and Young, Price Waterhouse (PwC) and KPMG are known as the Big 4 because they are among the largest public accounting firms in the world (at the time of this writing) and they are constantly looking for risk assessors, auditors and cybersecurity workers. If you are a certified public accountant (CPA), a bank teller or in the financial space this will actually help you work in cybersecurity with these guys.

Intelligence & government – If you are in the military, military intel as an analyst or dealing with lots of classified data, you should already know there is a need for a professional who can protect all aspects of intelligence information. From cryptographers, cybersecurity analysts, mathematicians and programmers, all aspects of cybersecurity are needed to protect classified information.

Exercise: Top Five Choices

Step 1: Look at the NICE Cyber Workforce jobs

Look at each category to get an idea of which ones best fit you. Is the "Oversee and Govern" a better fit because you have a business degree and have been managing for years? Are you excited about getting into doing technical hands-on in the "Operate and Maintain" category?

> Go to this site for more details on each category: niccs.cisa.gov/workforce-development/nice-framework

> Or check out book 2 of this series.

Step 2: Choose a specialty area

You need to go through each category and check out each special area. Write down which ones appeal to you most.

Step 3: Select work areas

Drill down into each specialty area and take notes of the work areas that you would like to do, seem fun, or seem like a good fit.

Step 4: Brainstorm jobs

With just a pen and pad write down all the jobs you would like to do. Don't worry about what is good or bad for now because you are going to let the ideas flood the page.

Step 5: Circle the top 5

On your list of jobs, choose five that stand out. You will either have a "good feeling" about them or have some connection to them. Maybe you have experience with them and you're surprised that they are were part of the special areas. Perhaps you have a friend who did that job and you know it's great. Whatever the reason you can only choose five so choose wisely.

Step 6: Study your top 5

There are three things we are going to look at for your top five jobs:

- Look at the industry of each job
- Look at the salary range of each job
- Find videos of people who talk about these jobs

The search engine is your friend. But your best resource is if you know someone who is already doing this job.

Find Keywords

Stop!

Do not start this chapter without your list of five jobs!

You should have an idea of job titles, industry, and places to find more information on these jobs.

This list of five is important because we will find keywords based on these jobs.

Before we start the resume, we should gather keywords on each of the areas you have chosen.

Gather job titles

Take the job titles you have written down and use job search engines to analyze the keywords found in posted positions and resumes.

For example, let's say you wanted to get into forensics. First of all, your research should have given you an idea of some of the job titles in this career path. Just typing in your job into a job search will give you a few. This is the first thing you need to do, gather job titles. You must use a job search site in the top ten of the country you want to work in.

In the case of forensics, we type "forensics" into indeed.com and immediately we see autocompletion show the following:

- Forensic science
- Forensic science technician
- Forensic scientist
- Forensic social worker

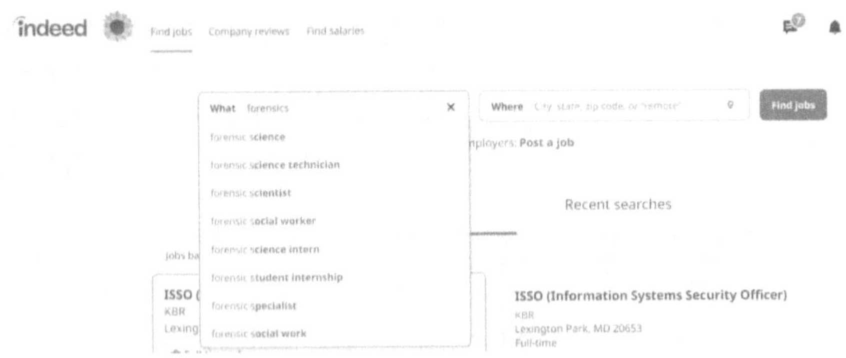

But we are looking for computer forensics. We need to narrow our search. We can actually type in "computer forensics" or we can use the NICE Cyber Workforce as a reference guide.

On the NICE framework resource, you can do a search for your job title, but the best way is to identify the category, navigate each specialty area and look up "Work Roles." We will explore this in detail in book 2, but for now check out the NICE framework summary in this book to get an idea of each category.

Forensics is under the "Investigate" category, which has a specialty area called "Digital Forensics." The work roles under this specialty include cyber defense forensics analyst and law enforcement / counterintelligence forensics analyst. Using these key phrases from the NICE framework, we can gather additional job titles from our top job search sites and we come up with this:

- Host cyber forensics
- Network cyber forensics
- Cyber defense forensics analyst
- Cybersecurity analyst
- Cybersecurity engineer
- Security operations center analyst
- Cyber threat analyst

You will notice that not all job titles are obvious. They don't all have the word "forensics" in the job title, but have it as a required skill in the job description. You will find this in some jobs you go after. This is because organizations can name the job title whatever they want. There is no standard for naming jobs, which is why you have job titles like "Digital Overlord," "Retail Jedi," "Wizard of Light Bulb Moments."

Key requirements, qualifications, and responsibilities

Now that we have an idea of what job titles are in digital forensics, we can start looking for requirements that employers are looking for.

Use any of the top job search sites and go down the list of job titles. We are going to look up jobs that have been posted in the last month.

In this example we are using "Cyber defense forensics analyst" jobs posted on Indeed.com in the last 14 days.

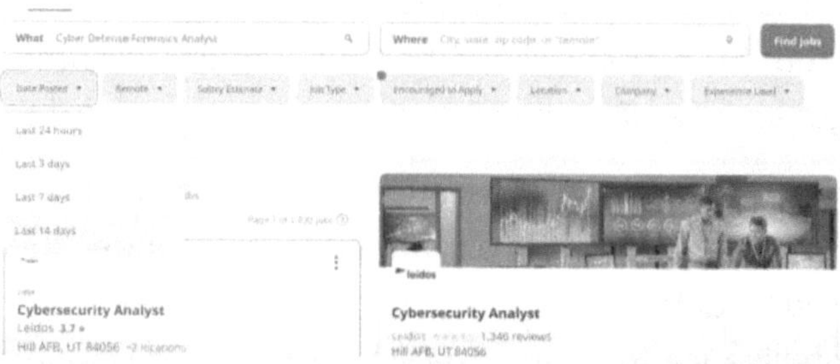

We will use multiple job titles from the list we gathered and we are looking at the last 30 days because we want the most current and accurate data from today's job market.

If you conduct this search and there are no results, choose another position title or expand the days.

We are looking for the requirements of the job to get an idea of what we should have on our resume and gather keywords.

Cyber Security Vulnerability Researcher, Forensic Analyst

KBR
Lexington Park, MD 20653
Full-time

Apply now

Required Qualifications:

EDUCATION

- Masters Degree in Cybersecurity, Computer Forensics or related field from an accredited college or university.

OR

TRAINING

- NEC 742A Network Security Vulnerability Technician

- NEC H10A Basic Cyber Analyst/Operator

OR

DOD 8570 CERTIFICATION

- Computer Hacking Forensic Investigator (CHFI)

- GIAC Reverse Engineering Malware (GREM)

AND

- 5 years of relevant experience:

OR

ON THE JOB TRAINING

- NAVEDTRA 43350 (Malware); with privileged access.

- NAVEDTRA 43469 Watchstation 303 Information Assurance Technician Level III

The very first results for our "Cyber defense forensics analyst" title say that the requirements include:

- a master's degree in cybersecurity or related field
- or training in network security vulnerability
- or a DoD 8570 certification
- or a computer hacking forensics investigator (CHFI)
- or GIAC Reverse Engineering Malware (GREM)

We need more keywords, so we will keep searching. The next job mentions "Basic Qualification" and "Responsibilities." I pulled data from five job requirements, responsibilities and qualifications to look for a pattern of what employers are looking for.

Using just "Cyber defense forensics analyst" as a search, I saw that many of the jobs are in the federal government, specifically the US Department of Defense. They are security operating centers. They are usually looking for someone who is eligible to obtain a security clearance or has one already. I noticed the wanted skills in host-based and network forensics, full packet capture, NetFlow. Another thing I noticed is that they wanted you to be knowledgeable in TCP/IP, IPS/IDS and SIEM tools.

The certifications they wanted included those mentioned on a document called DoD 8570. They mentioned Security+, CEH and GSEC to name a few. So, from here we would want to know what "8570" and each certification they mention is.

8570 refers to the Department of Defenses' list of approved IT certifications. Other federal organizations and contracting organizations have started to use this list to figure out what certifications a potential candidate should have. See Book 2 for more details.

Visual method of identifying keywords

Aside from just taking notes on the keywords as you find patterns in different jobs, another thing you can do is use word art. There are word art sites that allow you to upload words and get a visual representation that shows which words are used more.

Step 1. Copy the keywords from five job descriptions

Go to one of the top job aggregators and copy the primary responsibilities, requirements, basic qualifications, and preferred qualifications. You can copy then into MS Word, text, or Google Docs or whatever; you just need some way to copy them. You will need about five jobs, but if you can get more that works better as long as they are for the same type of job.

Step 2. Paste the job text into WordArt

Use WordArt.com or a site that is similar and paste the words you copied into the site.

For WordArt.com:

Click "Create"

Select "Import"

Paste the job text into the "Import words" message box

Click "Import words"

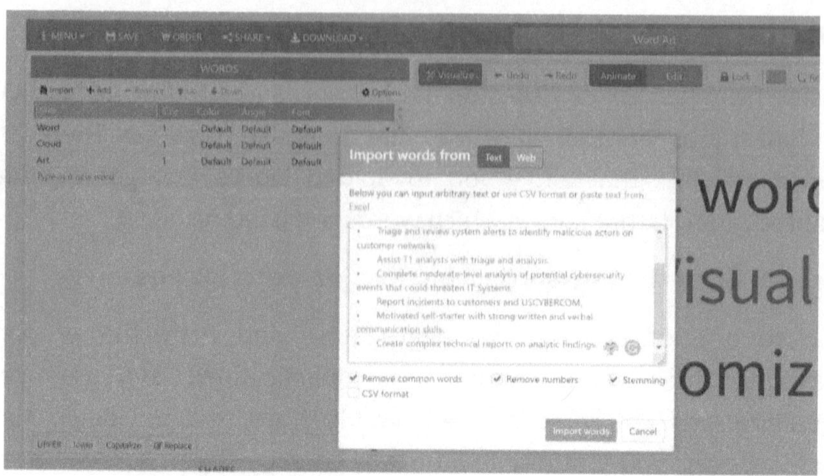

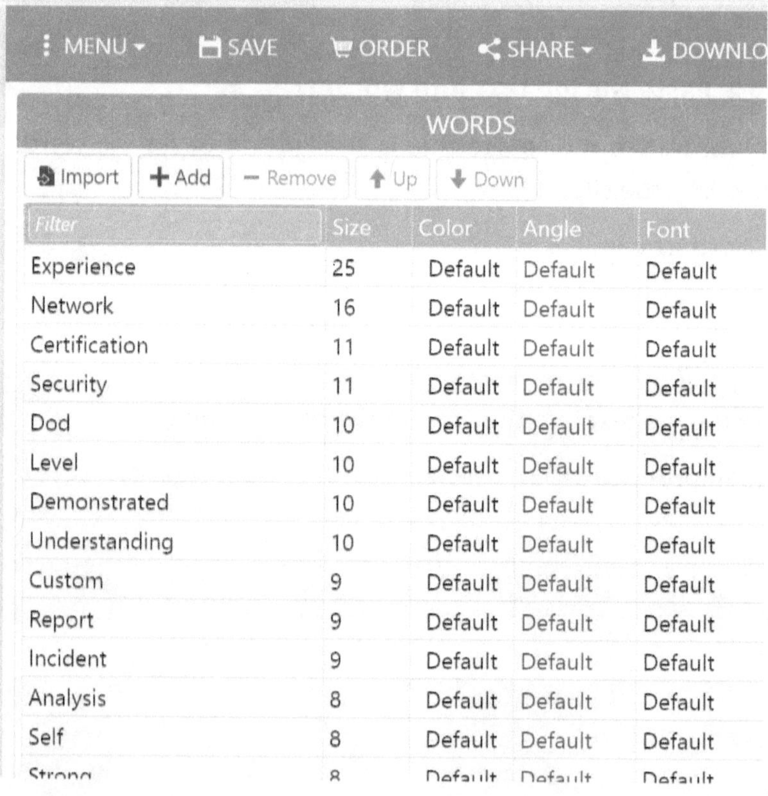

Filter	Size	Color	Angle	Font
Experience	25	Default	Default	Default
Network	16	Default	Default	Default
Certification	11	Default	Default	Default
Security	11	Default	Default	Default
Dod	10	Default	Default	Default
Level	10	Default	Default	Default
Demonstrated	10	Default	Default	Default
Understanding	10	Default	Default	Default
Custom	9	Default	Default	Default
Report	9	Default	Default	Default
Incident	9	Default	Default	Default
Analysis	8	Default	Default	Default
Self	8	Default	Default	Default
Strong	8	Default	Default	Default

Once you import words, the app will extract all of the keywords and show how many times each word is used across all of the text you uploaded.

Step 3. Create the WordArt

Click "Visualize" to create a visual representation of the data you copied. The larger the words in the word art the more it is used.

In our example, the largest words are *experience*, *certification*, *security* and *network*. Other words that are used multiple times include *demonstrate*, *understand*, *report*, *incident* and *analysis*.

This gives us an idea of where to focus because what we can do from here is put all these repeated individual words in context. We need to dig into what "experience" do they mean across each job. What "certification" are they looking for? We can find out by looking at notes that we used to copy and paste. Within our visual representation we need to look for specific cybersecurity keywords that will enhance our resume. We can see a few here for digital forensics:

- Create report
- Packet
- TCP/IP
- Incident
- Capture
- OSI
- Protocols

Looking at other peoples' resumes

The next thing we want to do is look at resumes of other professionals who are in the field we are searching. You can find these on LinkedIn. Do the same search for the position and job title but this time look for "People" instead of "Jobs."

Pay close attention to the top 20 professionals. Look at their profiles and what are they saying in their "About" section, the places they worked, and their experiences.

Work experience is really important since this section will have the most keywords and key phrases. Not all professionals make this information public so you may need to look at multiple LinkedIn profiles until you find one that is public.

Once you find a profile that has its work experience public, pay close attention to the keywords they put in their work experience. Read what they did in the position and the software and hardware they used (if any).

You are looking for patterns. You can use the word art trick on their resumes to get an idea of where to focus your search for key phrases. You will need to use at least three resumes and/or jobs in word art to get a good number of keywords. But the more you use the better the results. All the resumes, profiles and jobs you use need to be relevant to the job you are targeting.

Copy the way these top professionals word their experience in their respective fields. I am not telling you to lie on your resume and copy word for word what they did in their job. I am telling you to word your own matching experience similar to theirs. You will need to paraphrase and use your own style but use the exact same keywords.

Look for patterns

As you are reading through job descriptions, requirements and resumes in a specific area, you are looking for patterns. Once you read enough of them, you will notice that the same five or six IT certifications are popping up. You will notice whether or not degrees are necessary, if they can be replaced with experience or what types of degrees are needed.

Certain knowledge and skills will be repeated. You want to find those patterns and make your resume have some of those patterns.

Keywords with little or no experience

I don't encourage lying on your resume. And I am not telling you to copy skills and experiences that you don't have. If you have no experience at all in the area you are trying to go in, then this exercise is going to give you a very good idea of what you need to build to. You can still start building your profile, but you will need to start studying the basics and creating home labs to engage the common body of knowledge in information technology.

See appendix A, for a breakdown of each entry-level certification that I recommend.

Keywords in Work Experience

Work experience is important enough to deserve its own chapter (twice). This is where we can put in the most keywords. Work experience is where the technical recruiters and employers will spend most of their time if you are even considered for a position.

As we discussed, work experience in the ATS format requires a job title first, then the company, then location (optional) and finally the time frame in the following format – XX/XXXX (month/year).

Each role that you performed should have its own section.

Instead of paragraphs describing what you did at the positions, you must use bullets. So instead of paragraphs like this:

> Performed a vulnerability scan using Nessus across the network. This was part of a quarterly assessment of vulnerabilities with the vulnerability management team. This also helped the compliance of a critical system.

You will use bullets like this:

- Performed Nessus vulnerability scan for quarterly assessment
- Assisted vulnerability management team during mandatory assessments
- An essential part of the system security compliance effort on a critical mission system

The bullets are easier to process. It breaks out all the tasks individually to highlight each thing that you have done. The next step is to add impact to the actions you put in bullet form. It will look like this:

- Performed Nessus vulnerability scans for quarterly assessment of 100 mission essential systems; created dozens of reports for the decision-makers
- Assisted vulnerability management team during mandatory assessments to mitigate thousands of system vulnerabilities
- Created documentation as an essential part of the system security compliance effort on a critical mission system; was able to attain approval to operate three times

Cybersecurity action and impact

In order to get the employers to hire you as a cybersecurity professional, you have to put your cybersecurity skills on the resume.

If you have no experience in IT at all, this section will give you an idea of what experience you will need to build going forward. If you have any IT experience at all then there is a good chance that you already have some cybersecurity experience and you need to list it on your resume.

You can find cybersecurity experience in implementation, maintenance, configuration and monitoring. Security controls are the security features that protect the information system. This means everything from controlling physical access to encrypting the data to privacy procedures.

For any security controls that you have had anything to do with, you will need to provide the action performed and the impact on the organization. There will be times when you only mention the action, but the impact will really sell the action, so you want to add it whenever you can.

In order to get cybersecurity positions, the work experience should reflect all the security work that was done in your previous positions.

CIS critical security controls and best security practices

If you are trying to get a cybersecurity position, you will need to put the work you did applying CIS controls. If you have little or no experience and what to get a security position, then take notes because these are some of the things you can do to get your foot in the door.

The CIS security controls are a great place to figure out what cybersecurity skills employers are looking for. There are many other security compliance frameworks and control families we can use, such as NIST 800 or ISO 27001, but CIS is good for this type of breakdown. Formerly known as SANS critical security controls (SANS Top 20), they are now called the CIS critical security controls.

If you have applied, configured, reviewed or had anything to do with the following security controls, you need to have it on your resume:

- CIS Control 1: Inventory and Control of Enterprise Assets
- CIS Control 2: Inventory and Control of Software Assets
- CIS Control 3: Data Protection
- CIS Control 4: Secure Configuration of Enterprise Assets and Software
- CIS Control 5: Account Management
- CIS Control 6: Access Control Management
- CIS Control 7: Continuous Vulnerability Management
- CIS Control 8: Audit Log Management
- CIS Control 9: Email and Web Browser Protections
- CIS Control 10: Malware Defenses
- CIS Control 11: Data Recovery
- CIS Control 12: Network Infrastructure Management
- CIS Control 13: Network Monitoring and Defense
- CIS Control 14: Security Awareness and Skills Training
- CIS Control 15: Service Provider Management
- CIS Control 16: Application Software Security
- CIS Control 17: Incident Response Management
- CIS Control 18: Penetration Testing

CIS Control 01 & 02: Inventory and Control of Assets

In these controls the organization documents and tracks all their systems. This includes the software and hardware on desktops, internetwork devices and anything with an IP address connected to the network. This is important because if the organization does not know what is on its network, then they don't really have a secure system.

If you have participated in the control of assets, you might say something like this on your resume:

Activities:

- Conducted periodic hardware/software inventory assessments; tracked 1,000 assets in large environment.

- Maintained inventory of all equipment, software, and licensing

- Created and maintained a software/hardware inventory, network diagrams and assessment documents; resulted in 2 consecutive authorizations to operate packages

- Created SCCM reports and fine-tune software/hardware inventory to get customized reports for various audit purposes

- Coordinated activities in the organization related to ordering, receiving, storing, and distributing IT materials and equipment; important assets are distributed on time
- Utilized DPAS database to maintain accurate records for all 1,000 assets and to facilitate inventory controls and reporting requirements
- Responsible for investigating discrepancies and inventory shortages; recover $25,000 worth of critical equipment
- Worked directly with management to provide updates on stock inflow and outflow for effective decision making

- Assisted in development of procedures to keep inventory records accurate

CIS Control 03: Data Protection

Data protection is about more than just encryption. A data management plan will address what data is being stored and for how long. As well as who will access it, where it is stored and why it needs to be protected.

Work on data protection might include the following:

- Configured data access control lists based on a user's role; ensured 500 users and every system have access to exactly what they need
- Established and maintained the data inventory in accordance with the organization's data management process
- Enforced data retention in accordance with FISMA compliance
- Encrypted data on 500 end-user devices using Windows BitLocker and Apple FileVault; these mitigated risks associated with end-user devices being stolen
- Encrypted data on 500 removable media to protect against inadvertent data loss
- Implemented Transport Layer Security (TLS) and Open Secure Shell (OpenSSH) to encrypt sensitive data in transit
- Deployed a data loss prevention (DLP) tool to identify all sensitive data stored, processed, or transmitted through enterprise assets

CIS Control 04: Security Configuration of Enterprise Assets and Software

An organization must have control over their system's configurations. These are the security configurations of all assets and software.

If you have performed this security control then these might be the kinds of bullets that can help you:

- Established and maintained a secure configuration process for network infrastructure; the hardened 30 critical network devices include Cisco and Juniper devices
- Configured session locking on 210 servers and end-user systems; enabling session lockouts helped prevent unauthorized access to devices
- Implemented and managed host-based firewalls on over 700 mission essential systems
- Configured trusted DNS servers on enterprise assets; including configuring assets to use enterprise-controlled DNS servers and reputable externally accessible DNS servers
- Enforced automatic device lockout on mobile end-user devices
- Enforced remote wipe capability on over 2,000 portable end-user devices

CIS Control 05: Account Management

The organization needs to know who is logging in to their system and what credentials they have. If a person leaves the organization, they need to have a system that removes access to their user accounts. They also need to have a process that controls changes to the user's account. This is account management and it is a huge part of cybersecurity.

Here are the types of bullets you can use:

- Implemented strong password settings that are in line with CIS control best security practices
- Installed multifactor authentication (MFA) on a large enterprise with Linux and Windows systems
- Disabled dormant accounts to remove the likelihood of old accounts being exploited
- Created an account management policy that the organization uses to conduct account management on critical mission systems
- Restricted administrator privileges to dedicated administer accounts

CIS Control 06: Access Control Management

Access control means controlling logical access to information, systems, and objects in the environment. The organization must grant, refuse, and remove access in a standardized, timely, and repeatable way across an entire organization.

- Used active directory to enforce and maintain access control policies through the enterprise
- Granted and revoked access to enterprise assets for new hires, rights and changes to over 100 users
- Maintained role-based access controls on all 500 users in the organization
- Managed active directory for classified and unclassified environments with over 1,000 users and thousands of systems for 2 years

CIS Control 07: Continuous Vulnerability Management

Continuous vulnerability management has to do with vulnerability patching and checking. The continuous cycle is discovery of vulnerabilities, prioritization of vulnerabilities, resolution of vulnerabilities and repeating the process.

- Set up system-level alerting, including CVE detection on the enterprise for 100 critical systems

- Used the CVE program, Common Vulnerability Scoring System (CVSS), and organizations proprietary risk scoring methods to help manage and prioritize vulnerabilities

- Used Security Technical Implementation Guides (STIGs) and Security Content Automation Protocol (SCAP) Compliance Checker (SCC) to remediate the vulnerabilities on over 100 mission essential systems

- Applied knowledge of adversary tactics, techniques and procedures (TTPs), Cyber Kill Chain, Diamond Model for Intrusion Analysis, MITRE ATT&CK framework, CVSS, open-source intelligence (OSINT), or other relevant network defense and intelligence frameworks

CIS Control 08: Audit Log Management

Audit logs are gathered on servers, end-user systems, routers and other systems to detect, prevent and understand possible security incidents on the enterprise.

- Ensured that audit logs were enabled in a mixed mode environment that included Red Hat, Windows and MAC systems; allowed detection of over 100 threats against assets and improved cyber hygiene
- Configured audit log storage to make certain there was enough space for logs for mission-critical systems and

retention of log history in compliance with organizations 4 terabyte requirements

- Conducted 100 hours of security audit log analysis to detect anomalies or abnormal events that might match adversary tactics, techniques and procedures (TTPs) in the MITRE ATT&CK framework
- Retained 30 terabytes of audit logs across enterprise assets to satisfy audit and compliance needs.
- Experience with Linux/Unix based Information System Security requirements to include archiving audit log data using port 514

CIS Control 09: Email and Web Browser Protections

Since email and web browsers are the main way internal users interact with external and internal systems, it's important that the organization have protections in place. This means educating users on social engineering attacks and having antivirus tools installed and updated.

- Created training for all 70 employees on the proper usage of Web browsers and web-based products
- Updated signatures on enterprise antivirus software for the proactive protection of 1,500 end-point devices and servers on the LAN
- Set up DLP technologies like Proofpoint Email, DLP & CASB, Microsoft Information Protection (MIP), Microsoft Security Suite (Defender, DLP for OneDrive, and others)
- Conducted threat intelligence using endpoint detection and email threat protection; a crucial part of the incident response process
- Used DNS filtering services for all enterprise assets to block known malicious domains

- Placed restrictions on unauthorized client extensions for Chrome, IE, Firefox and other browsers as well as email clients
- Implemented DMARC policies to reduce the number of spoofed domains
- Managed email filter on the enterprise to restrict the risky file types to improve the security posture of the organization security posture

CIS Control 10: Malware Defenses

Every enterprise in an organization needs to have antivirus that protects all systems. The system will not constantly update in virus definitions and antivirus software.

- Deployed and maintained antivirus solutions on the organizations systems; protected 1,500 systems across the enterprise
- Disabled autorun and autoplay on 1,500 end-user devices for an extra layer of protection against malware that might be on removable media
- Provided support of the anti-malware program, forwarded alerts and warnings to users; created tickets for potential security incidents involving malware
- Continuously monitored server and firewall logs, as well as network traffic, to check for security incidents and traces of possible malware
- Installed antivirus and malware detection on thousands of mission essential systems

CIS Control 11: Data Recovery

Data recovery means prioritizing the data that needs to be stored, protecting the stored data and having a plan to recover it.

- Established and maintained the data recovery process of the organization for all critical data
- Performed scheduled tape backups on systems as required. Manage data backup library to include storage of tapes for 15 legacy systems
- Performed system backups and recovery on 10 mission-critical systems
- Performed system backups to ensure expedient restoration of the database for the respective network equipment
- Performed system backups to ensure expedient restoration of the database for the respective network equipment

CIS Control 12: Network Infrastructure Management

Networks are made up of information systems that must be configured, installed updated and maintained. Security must be put in place for internal, DMZ and external network systems.

- Created network diagrams and documentation for NIST 800 security compliance and network infrastructure management
- Established a secure network architecture by maintaining address segmentation, least privilege, and availability
- Maintained centralized network authentication, authorization and auditing (AAA) using Cisco router using Radius and TACACS+ protocols
- Used secure network management and communication protocols such as 802.1X, WIFI Protected Access 2 (WPA2) Enterprise
- Documented and controlled all ports, protocols and services on three network enclaves

- Created wired and wireless network designs on new networks
- Conducted provisioning, installation, configuration, and troubleshooting for network devices

CIS Control 13: Network Monitoring and Defense

Networks will have congestions, human errors, vulnerabilities and cyberattacks on a regular basis. Especially if the network has critical systems, has access to the Internet or has lots of users.

- Provided cybersecurity analysis on network traffic for the enterprise using tools like security information and event management (SIEM) tools such as Splunk
- Deployed a host-based intrusion detection solution on 600 end-user devices and 14 servers
- Experience detecting host and network-based intrusions via intrusion detection technologies like Snort and Splunk
- Experience implementing protocol analyzers Antivirus (AV) and Host Based Intrusion Prevention (HIPS)
- Deployed a network intrusion detection solution on enterprise assets on a large 15,000 system enterprise. This included a Network Intrusion Detection System (NIDS)
- Performed traffic filtering between network segments

CIS Control 14: Security Awareness and Skill Training

In an organization the ignorant users are the weakest link. All users who have access to the enterprise need to have a level of training equal to their level of access. This includes security awareness and skills.

- Taught security awareness to 400 employees in the organization resulting in users clicking on 30 percent fewer suspicious links during phishing campaigns

- Created basic training on mission essential systems, which included skills and security training for 45 personnel
- Trained 55 workforce members to recognize social engineering techniques such as suspicious phishing attachments and links and questionable calls
- Educated operational users on proper authentication best practices. This included creating strong passwords, password storage and the importance of screen locking
- Created guidance on protection of personally identifiable information and the causes of unintentional data exposure
- Gave training on how to identify and report security incidents
- Conducted role-specific security awareness and skills training

CIS Control 15: Service Provider Management

Most organizations have service-level agreements with multiple partners, vendors and service providers. In many cases, they are also service providers themselves. These services include cybersecurity consulting, vendor maintenance contracts, cloud, network, and management services. The organization must monitor and organize all service providers associated with their main mission or business. This is done with policy, service-level agreements, contract and other legal documents.

- Constructed a service-level agreement (SLA) for support of the organizations mission-critical services
- Updated the organization's service provider management policy to include additional services and remove those no longer necessary
- Ensured service provider contracts for network devices (Cisco IOS and Juniper) included security requirements
- Included PCI and SOC2 [regulation or framework] compliance with providers during assessment of service providers

CIS Control 16: Application Software Security

If an organization develops applications, they need to implement them securely using the software development lifecycles (SDLC). Even with web application ... especially with web applications, the organization needs to implement best security practices to protect users, clients and employee data being handled by the apps.

- Provided application security during the application development process; included vulnerability management, security of third-party code and application security testing procedures
- Implemented security software development framework (SSDF) during the software development process
- Processed and addressed software vulnerabilities discovered in application using scanning tools such as Nessus and Web Inspect
- Performed root cause analysis on security vulnerabilities discovered on software; identified patterns in the development process that created the vulnerabilities
- Maintained an inventory of third-party software components and ensured that any updates to components that are used in any part of SDLC are still compliant with the overall policies
- Analyzed the security posture of the organization applications with a severity rating system to determine the risk to the organization
- Used standard hardening configuration templates for applications and associated components including servers, databases, components, cloud containers, platform as a service (PaaS) component, and software as a service (SaaS) components
- Separated mission-critical production and non-production systems; this separation allowed the organization to have non-production testing environments to identify and remove vulnerabilities before putting them into production

CIS Control 17: Incident Response Management

All systems eventually have some sort of incident that renders the data on the system harder to access, corrupt, and modified in a way that was not authorized. There are incidents that take out a network, server or device or even cause sensitive information to be stolen. These incidents can be caused by accidents, malicious intent (criminal hackers) or nature. The organization needs to have a plan to respond to these incidents and that is where incident response management comes in.

- Critical part of the incident handling team; responded to 15 incidents on mission essential systems
- Established and maintained contact information for reporting security incidents involving potential malware on the network
- Assigned a key role and responsibility in the incident response process for the organization; responding to 5 security incidents
- Conducted after-action reports for incident response exercises on mission essential systems

CIS Control 18: Penetration Testing

Penetration testing includes having a team attempt to exploit vulnerabilities in networks, web apps and systems.

- Conducted penetration tests internally and coordinated with third parties for 7 organization assessments
- Developed processes and procedures to incorporate findings into vulnerability management programs for 5 clients and the organization
- Conducted vulnerability assessment testing and penetration testing for 4 clients
- Performed penetration tests and vulnerability assessments using the approved DoD vulnerability scanners (ACAS), Defense Information systems Agency (DISA) Security

Technical Implementation Guides (STIGs), Security Requirements Guides (SRGs) and other DoD software assurance security tools

- Used network analysis and penetration testing tools such as; Kali (BackTrack), Metasploit, Rapid 7 Nexpose, NMAP and Wireshark
- Conducted and document Security Test and Evaluation (ST&E) and physical security penetration tests on 5 mission systems

Create a Profile

At this point, you should have used relevant keywords for your targeted cybersecurity career path. You should have some of the CIS security controls and security best practices listed in your experience in action/impact bullets. One of the things you can do to make sure your cybersecurity ATS-style resume is solid is to run spell-check tools. You can also use a service like resumeworded.com or resumegenius.com that allows you to upload the resume so it can give you a quick free assessment. Make sure you run spell-check and proofread it start to finish.

Now that you have a solid cybersecurity resume, it's time to market it everywhere.

Before we start to market the resume, it is important that we gather all contact information that will be used on all the sites we are going to set up and the resumes we are going to make. This profile we are creating will act as notes. It will allow you to fill out the job site online profiles or give the cybersecurity job recruiters more information if they ask.

These notes are essential to every resume and online profile. It will help with privacy and organizing contacts once we turn on the marketing machine we will create.

Start with a blank page and add the following:

- First and last name
- Phone number
- Mailing address
- LinkedIn account (if any)

- Get a professional-looking photo of yourself – this will be used for online profiles on job sites
- Security clearances (if any)
- References (if any)

My profile example

Bruce Brown

(719) 838-3799

contact@convocourses.com

https://www.linkedin.com/in/bruce-cissp-rmf/

Security Clearance:

Active Secret (1/1/2017)

Active Public Trust level 6 (10/2/2019)

References:

James Smith – 720-456-0565

Jimmy Johns – +1 217-356-9900

Samantha Billingsly – 1888-0987

Your name

I use an alias on my resumes and profiles. This is completely optional so feel free to skip this step and use your real name. But the reason I use an alias is that it is too easy to find your personally identifiable information using just your real name and city.

If you don't live in the USA, then this might not be a problem for you. Perhaps your situation is different. But in the US, you can type your real name and city in Google and it will have the last few places you lived, phone numbers, people you are related to and all kinds of other information you might not know is listed publicly.

Again, if you have a different situation feel free to skip this step and use your real name.

Contact information

For contact information, you will need to provide an email, phone number and location. Use an email that is best for you but keep in mind you may get hundreds of emails from possible employers. Whatever email account you use, also make sure you check the spam and junk folders often as some legitimate potential employers will get sent there.

You will get so many calls and texts that you may not want to use your real phone number. It can get very annoying. What I sometimes do is use a free phone number and have the calls go to voicemail but it's up to you.

The best resource for a free phone number is voice.google.com. With voice.google you can have all calls forwarded to your personal phone, voicemail or you can block calls and make it so they don't interrupt your personal life. Once we turn on the resume marketing, you will get enough calls to interrupt your personal life.

Security clearances

If you have any security clearances, you can add them here along with their status and when they were active. This is useful information for screeners, during interviews and for your online profiles.

References

You will want to write these down on your profile page. Don't post them on your resume or your online profiles, this is specifically for you. Usually if they ask about it, employers are looking to validate your experience at positions that you have put on your resume. So, you can send them the list of references separately.

For the privacy of the people you will list, you don't want to add these references to your resume because it will be uploaded publicly all over the Internet. Instead, on your resume, you can put something like:

References

*References provided on request

Make sure you inform anyone you are listing as a reference and let them know when the employer will call them if you know this information.

Resume scammers

I created my profile in such a way that it gives me an extra layer of privacy and protection, but there are some things you should be aware of to protect yourself further.

Lately, there have been scammers that will find your resume and attempt to scam you to get your banking information or even hack the company you currently work in.

There are some work-from-home scams that will have you stuffing envelopes after paying a fee. And you make a commission by signing other people up. There are reshipping scams that will have you receive packages to reship them to another place, but they don't send you a paycheck.

There are online jobs that have you assemble products. They have you pay for all the raw material and pay a fee but they reject the finished product.

Recently, there have been some fake job offers that almost immediately ask for your personal information. Once they get this, they can possibly steal your money or identity.

There are some red flags that will let you know this is probably a scam:

Fee or payment requirements. Most legitimate jobs … correction, NO legitimate jobs I have ever had asked me to pay for anything. In fact, they will pay me for the pleasure of meeting me at the interview or pay my travel expenses if it is in another town. If someone is asking for a fee to even start their service do not do it. If you are starting your own business, yes. There are all kinds of startup costs, but for a job as an employee or contractor, no. There are no fees.

Download documents or files. There are some elaborate social engineering hacks that will have the criminal hacker pretend to be a technical recruiter, then have you downloaded malware. Do not click on any links or open any attachments anyone sends you. If they send you a document with the job description, scan it before downloading it. Do not download any files. If they send you a link, open a new browser and go to the site yourself. Or, better yet, go to the next potential job.

Early requests for sensitive information. It is not uncommon for employers to eventually get your social security number to conduct a background check. But normally, this is after you get an offer. This means you have been through more than one interview and talked to multiple people. And even then, you are entering your information into a secure site with an established background check organization. If they are asking for sensitive information too early, you should be suspicious. I have had technical recruiters ask me for my social security number the first time I talk to them. The answer is no.

The fake job offer that destroyed a multimillion-dollar organization

In 2021, a senior developer working for Sky Mavis applied for jobs. The company was OK to work for, but like all professionals, he was trying to level up and make more income.

Sky Mavis was doing very well. They'd developed a game called Axie Infinity. Axie Infinity was one of the first successful blockchain-based games that allowed players to make an income by playing. Avatars that gamers purchase to play have market value. In this game the avatars can be traded, bought and sold. Axie is like a Pokémon game where you can make money collecting, fighting and participating in the game! At one point the game had over 2 million active daily users and was making something like $15 million dollars per day. Some gamers were literally making a living with this "play to earn" model.

The senior software developer was approached by a company that encouraged them to apply for jobs on LinkedIn. They quickly had multiple rounds of interviews with increased difficulty.

After passing all the interviews, they were given a very generous offer. The offer was sent via a PDF.

The PDF was downloaded after signing up for the job offer. The company that did the interviews was actually a hacker group.

With the malware, the group was able to gain access to the Sky Mavis' network. The attackers went straight for the company's cryptocurrency wallet, which did not have adequate security. Sky Mavis lost $540 million dollars. This crippled the economy of Axie Infinity.

Further investigations revealed that the hacker group was associated with the North Korean government, which had successfully hacked another companies' cryptocurrency.

This is a cautionary tale for everyone in cybersecurity and IT. There are several ways that this could have been prevented. However, we won't go into how the organization did not have proper protection of their cryptocurrency infrastructure, or how there was very weak internal network security that should have caught this. We will just focus on what the job seeker can do to avoid this.

1. No downloads. Do not download anything from untrusted sources.
2. Scan downloads. If you feel you MUST download files from untrusted sources, scan anything you download and do not open it on a network with access to anything important (i.e., banking info, cryptocurrency wallets, sensitive information or corporate infrastructure).
3. Do not click random ass links. Do not click on links from untrusted sources sent via text, or email.
4. Scan links. If you have to click a link, you can check the link by copy/pasting it into a site like VirusTotal.com to check it for malware.

5. Too good. If the offer sounds too good to be true it probably is.
6. Conduct research on the company. Real companies will have a presence online and a number you can call to give you more information. Do not rush. Take your time to research the company. Find what employees have said about it. Find articles, press releases, and social media posts about the company.
7. Check the company's reputation. Check out the company's web page and see if the job is listed publicly. Sometimes they will have more information about the position and even the salary that they pay for it that they don't want to discuss in the interview.

In all my years of doing cybersecurity, getting hacked, seeing organizations get breached, conducting risk assessments, what I have learned is that anyone can "get it." That means anyone at any time can get scammed and victimized. No one, and I mean, no one, is exempt from getting scammed by clever attackers who have to take from you to gain anything. But for goodness sake, do not make it easy for them. Become a hard target.

Market the Resume

There is a passive and active side to marketing your resume. We are going to go through both of these.

Passive has two components: filling out the job site's profile and uploading your resume.

Actively market your resume has a few things you can do, but the main thing is applying for jobs.

Let's start with the passive side of marketing your resume.

Passive resume marketing

In this context, passive means you do something once and that work continues to bring results. In this case, the heavy lifting is done in your keyword research, resume building and filling out everything you need in the profile. If you have done your homework, then this will feel like a lot of copy and paste.

If you skipped all the keyword research and resume building, you will still need to do it.

Passive: online profiles and resume upload

Public Safety Announcement: If you created the profile in the last chapter, you will want to use that to help create the online profile. The last chapter was optional, but you have been warned. If you don't listen to what I am saying in this book, you only have yourself to blame when you get a million calls from all the call centers on earth. This shit works but you have to protect yourself, your privacy and your peace. OK. Let's get into this.

Most online profiles are about the same. They will ask for the same information and take about the same amount of time to do. Some of them can be filled out with your ATS-style resume and some are still manual. The more thorough you are with the online profile, the more attention it will get.

You will need to edit the online profile and fill out all sections with your resume information. Even if the job search site does this for you when you upload your ATS-style resume, you will still need to upload your image, add some skills, and find anything out that is not done automatically.

Set the resume you added to public. Most job sites allow you to set the resume to public or private.

Cybersecurity Jobs: Resume Marketing

LinkedIn profile public

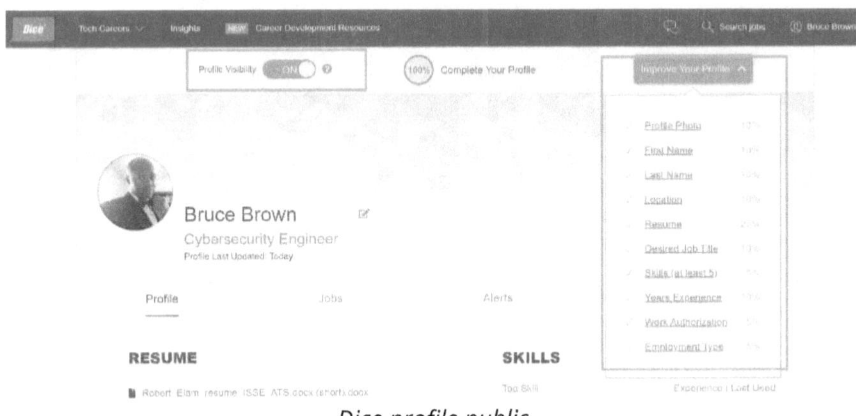

Dice profile public

Bruce Brown

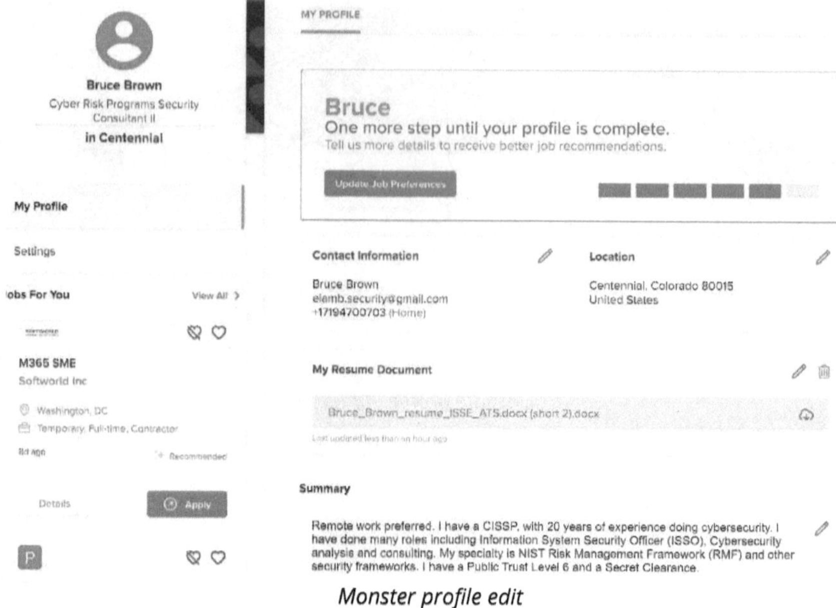

Monster profile edit

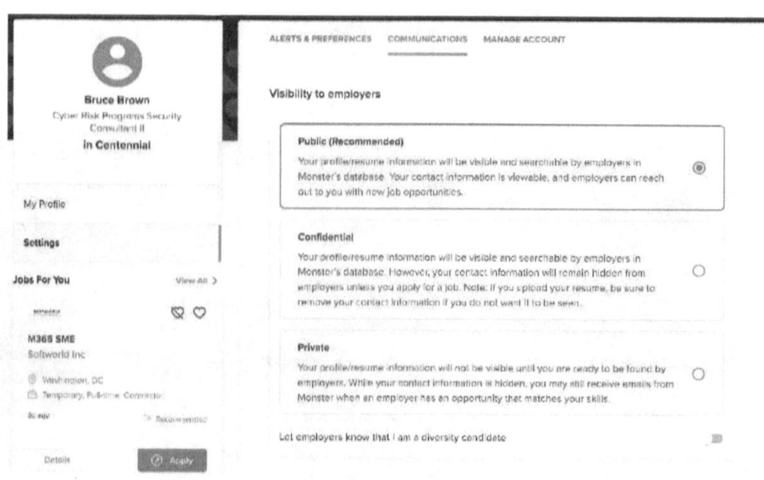

Monster profile public

All job search sites constantly change in style and usability. Links, features and buttons change but the most essential functions will be there. They will allow you to upload your resume, edit the profile to add more about yourself and allow you to make the resume public or private.

If you don't do these basic things, the job search will not be as effective. The online profile will usually give you an idea of what percentage of that you've completed. Get as close to 100 percent as possible.

Upload multiple resumes

You can also upload more than one resume to target different positions. For example, at one time I was a SIEM engineer and an ISSO. These are two different cybersecurity roles that have different certifications, experience and requirements. So, I create a resume for each.

Post your resume everywhere

You need to upload your resume to as many job search engines as possible. You never know which one will work for you. I get the most messages and interaction from LinkedIn, but most jobs I actually interview for are from Monster and Dice and every now and then I will get an incredible job offer from a random job aggregator that I forgot that I posted to.

Post jobs in at least the top 6 job aggregators sites. But the more you do the better your results will be.

Post your resume at the organizations in your industry

Find the organizations that are most dominant in your industry and apply for them. If your path is in the financial industry then you want to apply for the Big 4 account firms (Deloitte, PwC, KPMG, and Ernst and Young). You need to post your resume on their actual career sites. In the health-care industry, search for the top health-care companies.

At the time of this writing, the top health-care organization in the USA are:

- CVS Health Corporation

- UnitedHealth Group Incorporated

- McKesson Corporation

- AmerisourceBergen Corporation

All these companies need cybersecurity and IT professionals.

Your research will reveal where most of the jobs are for your cybersecurity category, specialty area or work role. For example, as an information system security officer (ISSO), I know that most of the jobs are in the federal government. What I do is search for the top government contract companies. Then I go to their career page and upload my resume.

Security clearance tips

There are job sites that specialize in government positions and jobs that require a security clearance. One great thing about these job site profiles is that they usually have a section for security clearances. If you have a security clearance, you will want to add it here. Here are some job sites that specialize in security clearance jobs.

- USAJobs.gov
- Clearancejobs.com
- Clearedcareers.com
- Silent professionals

There are many kinds of clearances but the ones you see most often in the USA are: Confidentiality, Secret and Top Secret clearances. You must be a US citizen to be eligible for these. There are positions of "public trust" but this is not considered a security clearance. So, although there is a background check, the candidate does not need to be a US citizen. Public trust background checks are often required for IT or financial positions supporting the government. They don't go as deep as clearances, but they do look at some of the following:

- Misconduct in employment

- Criminal conduct

- Deception or fraud in examination or appointment

- Refusal to furnish testimony as required for the investigation

- Alcohol abuse

- Illegal substances, without evidence of substantial rehabilitation

- Involvement with attempts to overthrow the US government by force

I am always asked, "how can I get a security clearance?"

First of all, a security clearance is not required for all cybersecurity jobs. The word "security" in security clearance is misleading. A security clearance allows an individual filling a specific position to have access to sensitive information. This can include positions like secretary, courier and many others.

If you want a clearance you have to get one directly from the government or from a contract. If you are a US citizen, some organizations will actually get you a security clearance if it is necessary for the job. These are obtained based on the needs of a contract with a governing organization.

For more on US clearances check out dcsa.mil

Passive: profile alerts and algorithms

Once your online profile is complete the site will do some of the work for you. The job site's algorithm will find jobs that match your resume then suggest jobs to you. They will also suggest your resume to employers. Some sites also allow you to set up email or SMS alerts that will notify you whenever a job matches your resume.

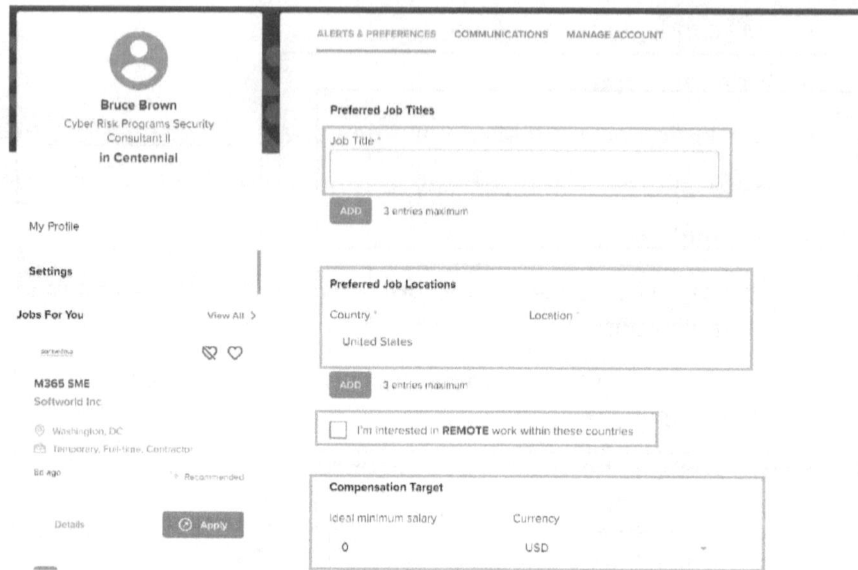

Active: applying for jobs

The active side of your campaign consists of applying for jobs on all the sites that you have profiles on. If you have filled out your profile completely, you will start getting pop-ups of jobs that fit your skills and experience.

You need to search for jobs using your keywords. You will see many jobs. But we need to filter the search to find the most relevant jobs. There are a few filters that you must apply on job sites. Here is how it looks on LinkedIn:

- Filter by jobs
- Search for jobs that are within the last month or two weeks
- Choose "Easy Apply"
- Search "Experience Level"

Cybersecurity Jobs: Resume Marketing

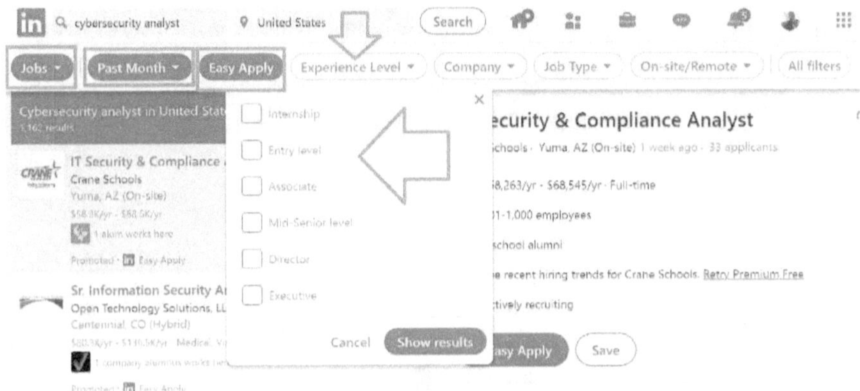

LinkedIn job search filters

On Dice.com you will do the same thing. Use your keywords to search for jobs, filter by a date range so it will only show recent jobs posted and choose "Easy Apply."

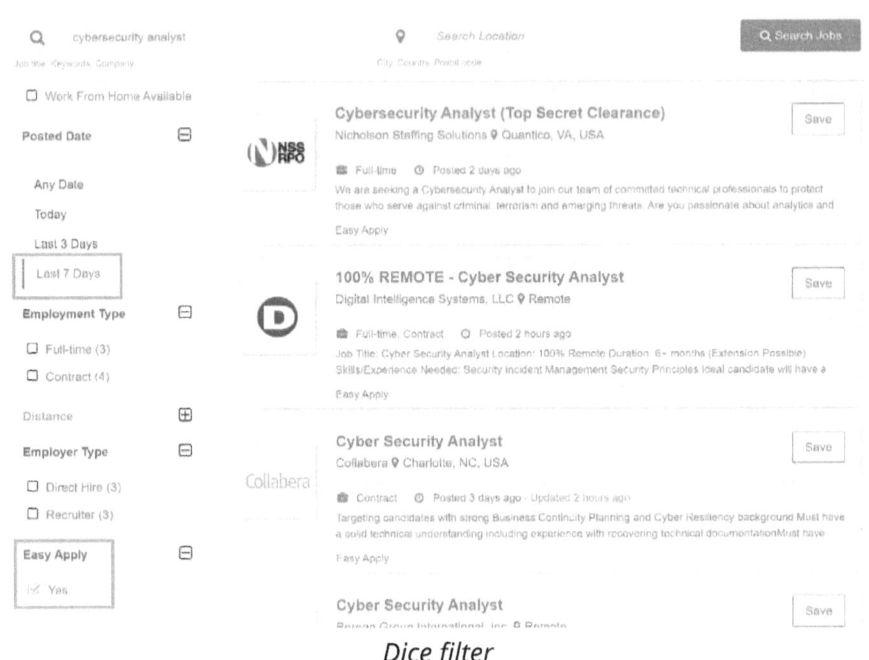

Dice filter

On moster.com, there is the same kind of filter for your job search.

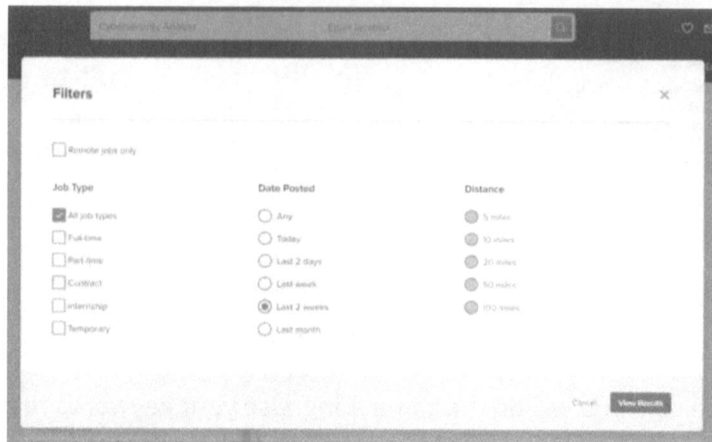

Monster.com also has a "Quick Apply" feature.

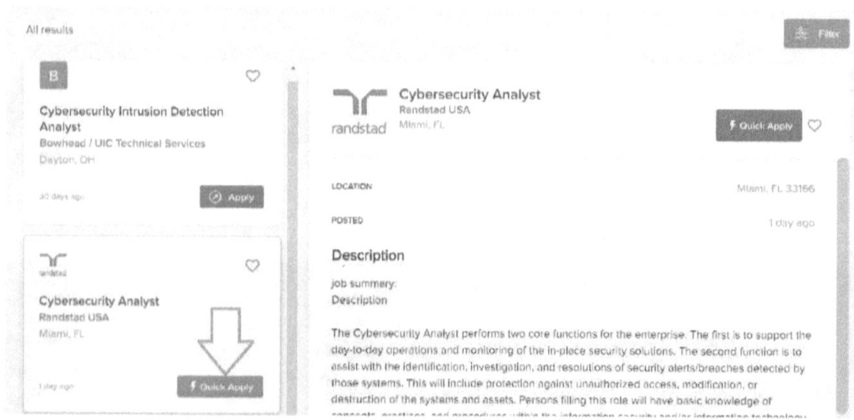

"Quick Apply" and "Easy Apply" features allow you to apply with just a few clicks because it pulls in data from your complete online profile. But the profile needs to be filled out properly and you need to upload your ATS-style resume. Many job sites will have this type of feature.

Conclusion: You Will Get a Lot of Messages and Calls

If you have taken action by doing deep keyword research, updating your ATS-style resume and doing passive and active marketing then you will get some contacts, opportunities and maybe even some job offers.

Results will vary. So much relies on your experience and skills in IT and cybersecurity. But even if you have no experience, this guide can serve as a map to plan where you want to go in your career. For example, if you know that you want to do digital forensics then your research will tell you what you need to do. You will need to study for it. But now you have a blueprint for you what you need and what the employers want.

Appendix A: Entry Level Certs

If you have ZERO IT experience you need to gain the skills and knowledge that can get you into an entry-level IT position. Going to University or community college is a great way to start. But there are pros and cons.

The pros of going to college are that some schools offer the skills and IT certifications in their degree programs; a degree is one of the best things you can have on a resume (for IT and cybersecurity jobs you will want to get a degree in STEM – science, technology, engineering, or mathematics).

The cons of going for a degree are that it can be expensive, it's very slow, colleges rarely teach exactly what you will be doing on the job (most of the good stuff you'll learn on your own).

Aside from pursuing a degree, there are some entry-level certifications that will get your foot in the door. IT certifications are actually supposed to validate the skills you already have, but the curriculum is so good on certifications that you can use it to build your knowledge and skills as you study for the tests.

There are many entry-level IT certifications out there. But there are a few entry-level certifications I would recommend based on their marketability, salary range and what they teach.

At the time of this writing, Comptia.org, Amazon and Google have the hottest entry-level certifications.

You can start with entry-level IT certifications. Here are a few that I would recommend you start with.

- Google IT Support Professional
- CompTIA +ITF
- CompTIA A+
- AWS

Google IT Support Professional

The Google IT certificates do not require relevant experience. At the time of this writing, there are two Google IT certificates available: introductory IT Support Certificate and an advanced-level IT Automation with Python certificate.

IT courses included in the IT Support program are:

- Technical Support Fundamentals
- The Bits and Bytes of Computer Networking
- Operating Systems and You: Becoming a Power User
- System Administration and IT – Infrastructure Services
- IT Security: Defense Against the Digital Dark Arts

Courses in the IT Automation with Python curriculum include:

- Crash Course on Python
- Using Python to Interact with the Operating System
- Introduction to Git and GitHub
- Troubleshooting and Debugging Techniques
- Configuration Management and the Cloud
- Automating Real-World Tasks with Python

Both courses are on Coursera.com for a monthly subscription of $39 USD (at the time of this writing).

This IT certificate is still pretty new compared to the other entry-level certifications. While there are some jobs that only require these Google support certificates, there are not many. Set up an alert on the job search sites to capture these jobs as they are posted.

As of 2019 the median annual wage for this certification was about $55,000. The salary will vary based on other certifications, any experience and location of the job.

If you really want to level up in your IT or cybersecurity career, eventually you will need to really consider some sort of degree program.

CompTIA Certifications

The CompTIA A+ certification was the first IT certification that I earned. The first certification will probably be your hardest because you're nervous and you have to get used to the types of questions. CompTIA certification, particularly the A+ and Security+, are very well known in every industry. CompTIA has four areas of certifications:

- Core
- Infrastructure
- Cybersecurity
- Data and analytics
- Professional

I recommend you stick with core if you have no experience and don't know much about IT. These are all entry-level certs that can get you on the path to getting your first IT position. The top entry-level CompTIA certs are:

- A+
- Security+
- Network+

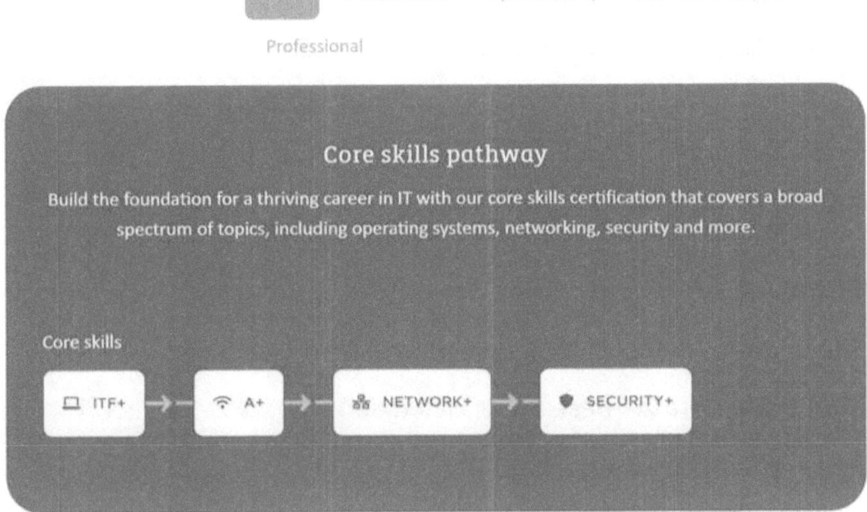

I would recommend the CompTIA A+. It will build your knowledge base of how information technology works. But if you feel like it might be too much, there is another certification that is more of an introduction. It's called the CompTIA ITF+.

CompTIA ITF+

Information Technology Fundamentals+ (ITF+) allows you to get familiar with basic IT knowledge and skills. It is for students preparing to enter the IT workforce and professionals changing to IT or IT-related fields. This certification is great if you don't even know if you want to get into IT yet. A+ certifications are a much larger commitment. The test is more expensive in time spent studying and money. ITF+ is specifically designed as a pre-career certification because it focuses on a broader understanding of IT for nontechnical professionals. It covers the following areas:

- IT concepts & terminology
- Infrastructure
- Applications & software
- Software development
- Database fundamentals
- Security

The test consists of 75 multiple-choice questions.

CompTIA A+

The CompTIA A+ consists of two separate certifications,

Core 1 and Core 2. These are updated about every 2–3 years.

A+ covers the following:

- A+ Core1 – mobile devices, networking technology, hardware, virtualization and cloud computing
- A+ Core 2 – operating systems, security, software and operational procedures

Both exams are 90 questions and multiple choice. Candidates must complete both exams to attain the A+ certification. According to payscale.com, the average CompTIA A+ holder has an average base salary of $66,000/year. But you have to factor in other things such as no experience, degrees and other certifications to get a more accurate view of the salary.

This also depends on the title, company and location. If you are getting the A+ certification as your first certification with no experience, your main goal is to gather experience so you can level up later. It is one of the most popular entry-level IT certs in the current market.

From the A+ cert, I would recommend going straight into Network+ or Security+ or both.

CompTIA Network+

I took this certification after I took the A+. Although it is not as marketable, it helps me to have a better understanding of networking concepts and the associated technology. Another good thing about the Network+, is that it is not vendor specific like other network certifications (i.e., Cisco & Juniper).

Network+ covers the following areas:

- Network fundamentals
- Network implementation
- Network operations
- Network security
- Network troubleshooting

CompTIA Security+

Security+ is one of the top 10 security certifications you can get in the industry. It is highly marketable. Because it covers so many requirements on the DoD 8140 approved certification list, it is on many contract job requirements.

Security+ covers:

- Attacks, threats and vulnerabilities
- Architecture and design
- Implementation
- Operations and incident response
- Governance, risk and compliance

There are 90 multiple choice and performance-based questions.

AWS Certified Cloud Practitioner

Cloud is a super-hot subject in IT and cybersecurity right now. Just having this certification will get your resume looked at. This certification is intended for anyone who has basic knowledge of the Amazon AWS platform. They expect you to have six months of exposure to the AWS cloud, basic understanding of IT services and their uses in a cloud platform as well as knowledge of core AWS services and use cases, billing and pricing models, security concepts and how cloud impacts business. For this reason, you should probably go for the A+ certification, network+ and maybe server+ first.

This is a 65-question multiple choice test.

Cybersecurity Jobs & Career Paths

Book 2

Find Cybersecurity Jobs

By

Bruce Brown, CISSP, ISC2 CAP

Hacking = Cybersecurity?

There is a lot of interest in cybersecurity, but people think that it's all about hacking. In this book I want to show you that there are many categories of this career path that have nothing to do with hacking or coding.

TV and movies glamorize this one aspect of cybersecurity and it's so ingrained in people's minds that they think that hacking is cybersecurity.

I have been doing cybersecurity and IT since the year 2000 and I want to inform you that there is a lot more to cybersecurity than cracking passwords, infiltrating a school's system to change the grades or breaking into the databases of banks and police departments.

Cybersecurity includes creating encryption modules, meeting laws and regulations of countries, and industries. It also involves intelligence and analysis of network traffic, analysis of software code and securing digital evidence for a criminal case. Because computers have to be in an environment that is controlled, cybersecurity also includes some physical and personnel security. You have to control who has physical security to the systems.

Cybersecurity is important for every aspect of information technology from the initial design of a computer system to a system's end of life. Computer hacking is a small percentage of what cybersecurity is. In fact, what is hacking? The Oxford dictionary defines it as the act of "gaining unauthorized access to data in a system or computer." This is a very limited definition of the term. What cybersecurity professionals consider "hacking" is a pretty broad field that includes, penetration testing, red teams, black hats, gray hats, white hats, phreakers, social engineering and others.

Cybersecurity is a huge field that requires more than just clever hackers who can crack a database. We need skilled communicators, leaders, managers, and analysts from all walks of life. Not all cybersecurity professionals are even technical.

With this book, my hope is for you to understand the breadth of opportunities available in the cybersecurity field by broadening your understanding of the term.

If you want to know more about cybersecurity as a whole join us on:

- convocourses.com
- youtube.com/convocourses
- convocourses.podbean.com
- facebook.com/convocourses
- Tiktok.com/@convocourses

Overview of Cybersecurity Field

Some people in the industry make a distinction between information security and cybersecurity. They describe information security as focused on protecting an organization's confidentiality (secrets), integrity (authorized modifications), and availability. While cybersecurity is focused on cybercrimes, cyber fraud, law enforcement and threats on "cyber space".

By these definitions, I have done both cybersecurity and information security. And I am telling you it's a waste of time to debate the differences because there is just too much overlap. As a "cybersecurity person" you will secure information and as an information security person you must be aware of laws, cybercrimes and threats from "cyber space". Also, the US federal government and states use the terms interchangeably. The only people that want to draw a line in the sand between cybersecurity and information security are geek bloggers online who have too much time on their hands.

So in the interest of getting to the point, we will call the entire field cybersecurity and then define the categories, areas and role under one giant circus tent.

With that out of the way, let's proceed.

Cybersecurity has work that is technical, managerial, analytical, and scientific. There are some jobs that have a spectrum with some combination of each of these.

We will be using the National Initiative for Cybersecurity Education (NICE) Framework. It provides a common definition of cybersecurity, a comprehensive list of cybersecurity tasks, and the knowledge, skills, and abilities required to perform those tasks.

As comprehensive as it is, even the NICE Cybersecurity Workforce Framework misses some parts of the cybersecurity spectrum, so we will fill in the blanks with the "information security color wheel".

Information Security Color Wheel

Government, health care, financial and other organizations have adopted the term "Red Team", "Blue Team and "Purple Team" to refer to offensive and defensive security roles.

> **Red Team** – Offensive security. These are cybersecurity professionals tasked with testing the resilience of a system or network against real attacks.

> **Blue Team** – Defensive security. Cybersecurity professionals tasked with detecting, defending and fighting against cybersecurity attacks. Blue team tasks are covered extensively in Protect and Defend and other categories of the NICE Cybersecurity Workforce.

> **Purple Team** – Improve the security posture. Red and Blue make purple. Purple team combines the perspective of both attackers and defenders. Individuals in this area create reports and analyze the data from offensive and defensive activities so that they can help the leadership of the organization become more secure.

Cybersecurity professional April Wright presented a more in-depth breakdown of the color schemes information security wheel at Black Hat USA 2017 cybersecurity conference that included more roles. She expanded on the cybersecurity color "team" concept, by introducing a spectrum:

> **Yellow Team** – Software developers, system architects and engineers. These are positions tasked with building the

infrastructure everyone is working on. The chapter on "Operate and Maintain" goes into these positions.

Green Team – Combination of Blue Team defense and Yellow Team builders. They enhance the security features with design and code.

Orange Team – Orange is a combination of the Red Team, who discover holes in the network, and Yellow who need to be aware of the weaknesses in the networks and systems they build. They educate and create awareness around the security vulnerabilities and risks to the organization.

White Team – These are the people tasked with coordinating the offensive and defensive activities. They will setup, document and get authorization for the penetration testing and ethical hacking that goes into the offensive Red Team activities. The White Team also documents and assesses the controls and activities of the defensive Blue Team. The NICE Cybersecurity Workforce goes into greater detail about this field of work. Their work roles include governance, risk, compliance (GRC), risk management, security control assessors, information system security managers and other compliance, management and risk analysis type positions.

April Wright (@aprilwright) is one of the cybersecurity professionals credited with the clever blending of skills using primary colors. It's a great way to explain cybersecurity roles and how they work together to protect an organization's assets.

Cybersecurity Workforce Categories

The National Institute for cybersecurity careers and study (NICCS) is managed by the Office of the Chief Learning Officer (OCLO) within the Cybersecurity and Infrastructure Security Agency (CISA).

NICCS promotes cybersecurity awareness, education, and career advancement throughout the USA. Their mission is "to be a national resource/hub for cybersecurity education, careers, and training." For more information about NICCS go to https://niccs.cisa.gov/.

NICCS created the National Initiative for Cybersecurity Education (NICE) cybersecurity workforce framework.

NICE Cybersecurity Workforce Framework gives a good breakdown of the categories of cybersecurity and the associated tasks, knowledge, and skills that are needed to perform the work.

Cybersecurity Workforce Categories

The Cybersecurity workforce has a comprehensive breakdown of cybersecurity categories, specialty areas and work roles. The categories divide up general functions important to security in information technology as a whole.

Each of these categories have areas of expertise known as "specialty areas". Within each specialty area are jobs or "work roles". The categories are a good way to understand which direction you want to go if you are interested in a cybersecurity career path.

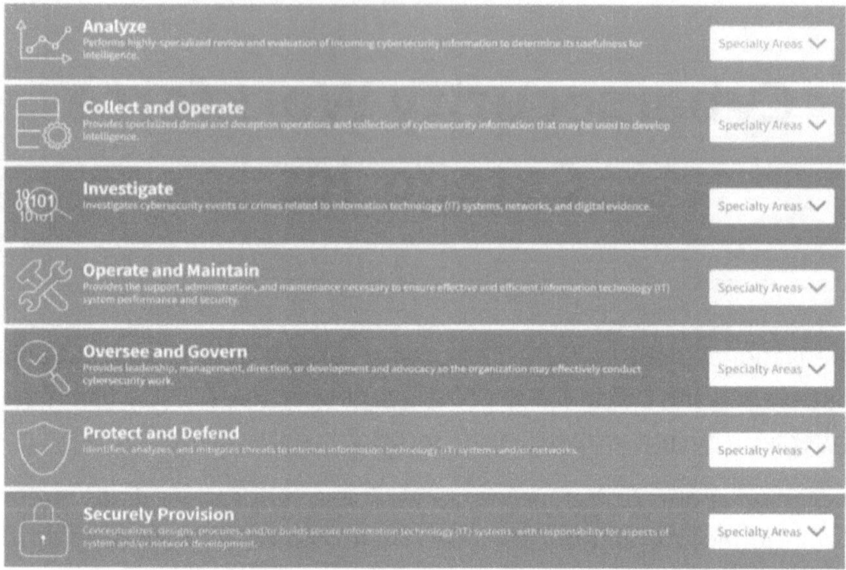

The 7 categories breakout into over 30 specialty areas and over 50 work roles. Realistically, the work roles are limitless because they are created by each organization.

As you go through each of the specialty areas, you will notice many work roles that are not cybersecurity by themselves, but are absolutely critical to cybersecurity as a whole. For example, program management and legal advice are not specifically technical or cybersecurity positions, but without a subject matter expert in these areas, implementing effective cybersecurity is not possible in certain situations.

This is why it is important to understand that cybersecurity is not just hacking and penetration testing. An organization needs more than a firewall and use of Nmap to have comprehensive security and defense in depth to protect their assets, reputation, human resources, business and mission. Cybersecurity is in every part of the organization's structure. And you can be an active part of it.

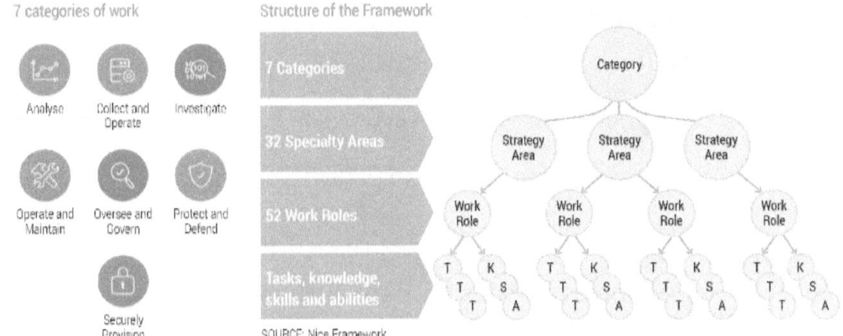

The NICE Cybersecurity workforce categories include:

- **Securely Provision** – architect and design secure information systems. Securely Provision has the following specialty areas:

    o Risk Management

    o Software Development

    o System Architecture

    o System Development

    o Systems Requirements Planning

    o Technology R&D

    o Test & Evaluation

- **Oversee and Govern** – manage and guide the organization so they can effectively conduct cybersecurity. The areas of expertise include:

    o Cybersecurity Management

    o Executive Cyber Leadership

    o Legal Advice and Advocacy

    o Program / Project Management and Acquisition

    o Strategic Planning and Policy

- o Training

- **Protect and Detect** – identify and analyze threats to internal information systems and networks. The specialty areas are:
  - o Cyber Defense Analysis
  - o Cyber Defense Infrastructure Support
  - o Incident Response
  - o Vulnerability Assessment and Management

- **Collect and Operate** – gather cybersecurity information that may be used to develop intelligence. Collect and Operate have the following specialty areas:
  - o Collection operations
  - o Cyber operational planning
  - o Cyber operations

- **Investigate** – investigate security events or crimes related to information technology. Investigate only has two specialty areas:

    o   Cyber investigation (cybersecurity analyst)

    o   Digital Forensics

- **Operate and Maintain** – provide support, administration and maintenance to ensure effective and efficient information systems performance and security. Operate and Maintain has these IT specialties:

    o   Customer services / technical support

    o   Data administrator

    o   Network services

    o   System administrator

- **Analyze** – review and evaluate incoming cybersecurity information to determine its usefulness for intelligence. The specialty areas are:

    o   Exploit analysis

    o   Threat Analysis

    o   Targets

    o   All-source analysis

These categories include management, policy, administrative technical, analytical and many other types of positions.

All US federal agencies rely on this framework. This includes the Department of Defense. The DoD created an approved baseline of certifications that is based on the Cybersecurity workforce framework (see Appendix A for more information).

We will be covering each of these categories in detail and giving insight into what the cybersecurity market wants you to do to get positions that are within these categories.

The "Analyze" Category

According to the cybersecurity workforce framework, someone within the "Analyze" category "performs highly-specialized review and evaluation of incoming cybersecurity information to determine its usefulness for intelligence."

In other words, professionals in this category review and evaluate information to figure out if the organization needs to take action.

Some real world examples of this would be a cybersecurity analyst in a security operation center (SOC). They monitor data and have to determine if the information is a security incident. They read system logs and need to determine if there is a pattern that indicates a cyberattack or the presence of malware in the environment.

Professionals in this category make anywhere from 70K USD to 120K USD annually.

The Cyber work force document lists five specialty areas:

- All-source Analysis

- Exploitation Analysis

- Language Analysis

- Targets

- Threat Analysis

All-Source Analysis

From the NICCS cyber workforce, this specialty area analyzes threat information from multiple sources, disciplines, and agencies across the Intelligence Community (IC). They gather intelligence and put it in context to gain insight about the possible implications.

Work roles under this specialty area pulls data from event logs, news feeds, and sensitive intelligence sources using applications, services and other methods. They gather all this data together to support missions and operations. These intelligence analysts are weaving together information from many sources to present a larger picture that might not be obvious at first glance.

The analyst must be able to communicate complex information, collaborate with teams, analyze large sets of data and think like a threat actor. An analyst has extensive and in-depth knowledge. They need to have a very good understanding of computer networks, cyber threats and exploitation as well as TCP/IP, virtualization and many other technologies.

When I worked at the SOC the most important skills were understanding networking (the TCP/IP three-way hand-shake), different types of hacks and exploitation of vulnerabilities and the incident response process. The very best people in this job had relevant training, certifications, experience or degrees that focused on identifying and handling security incidents. Some of the top certifications and training comes from the SANs organization. SANS has the GIAC Certified Intrusion Analyst certification (GCIA) and the GIAC Certified Incident Handler which really stand out as some of the best training you can get for this specialty area. These certifications validate a practitioner's knowledge of network and host monitoring, traffic analysis, and intrusion detection. The GCIA certification includes knowledge of advanced analysis and network forensics, concepts of TCP/IP and the Link Layer, DNS, IP Headers, Tcpdump filter and many other skills.

See *giac.org* for more on analyst certifications.

The job roles include All-Source Analyst and Mission Assessment Specialist. A deeper dive on the job sites shows many other work roles including:

- Information System Security Officer

- Information Security Auditor

- Information Security Analyst

- Incident Analyst

- Cyber Analyst

- Threat Analyst

- All Source and Threat Analyst

Exploit Analysis

This specialty area analyzes information to identify vulnerabilities and potential for exploitation. Subject matter experts on Red Teams conducting offensive security fall into this area. This specialty is usually part of tasks associated with security operation centers. Work roles that conduct this task include:

- SOC Analyst
- SOC Engineer
- Cyber Security Analyst
- Cyber Security Test Engineer
- Penetration Tester
- Cyber Network Exploitation (CNE)

Tasks of exploit analysis include creating comprehensive exploitation strategies that identify exploitable technical or operational vulnerabilities. Exploit specialist sometimes require penetration testing or hacking certifications. These include but are not limited to:

- EC Council - Certified Ethical Hacker (CEH)
- EC Council - Licensed Penetration Tester (LPT)
- Infosec Institute - Certified Penetration Tester (CPT)
- Infosec Institute - Certified Expert Penetration Tester (CEPT)
- Infosec Institute - Certified Mobile and Web Application Penetration Tester (CMWAPT)
- Infosec Institute - Certified Red Team Operations Professional (CRTOP)
- CompTIA PenTest+
- Global Information Assurance Certification (GIAC) Penetration Tester (GPEN)
- GIAC - Exploit Researcher and Advanced Penetration Tester (GXPN)
- Offensive Security - Offensive Security Certified Professional (OSCP)

Although OSCP certification is among the highest levels, the government gives the most attention to CEH and GPEN exploitation certifications. The marketability changes constantly with certifications.

Language Analyst

This specialty area applies language, cultural, and technical expertise to support information collection, analysis, and other cybersecurity activities.

Work roles include Multi-Disciplined Language Analyst. These people analyze language and culture to gain more insight into information and situations. Their expertise might include interpretation of criminal activity, terrorist threats, helping to decipher messages and comments in malicious software, or translating messages on the Dark Web. They have tools like language databases to support their analysis and they specialize in specific languages. Their positions are very necessary in intelligence. If you know more than one language, this might be a specialty area for you to consider. Languages that are in demand in the USA include: Farsi, Chinese, Russian, and Korean.

If you are multilingual, this is definitely a skill you must list on your resume because you never know what organization might need you as a language specialist

Targets

This specialty area applies current knowledge of one or more regions, countries, non-state entities, and technologies. One of the job titles in this specialty area includes: "Target Developer".

A Target Developer has a group of tasks and skillsets that are critical in some security operations centers. These tasks include figuring out where criminal hackers are likely to attack. They do this by performing target system analysis and coordinating with intelligence organizations to validate which systems are being attacked or likely to be attacked. This specialty area can be part of SOC engineering or cybersecurity analysis.

Threat Analysis

Threat Analysts identify and assess the capabilities and activities of cybersecurity criminals or foreign intelligence entities. They also produce findings to help initialize or support law enforcement and counterintelligence investigations or activities.

Work roles include:

- Cybersecurity Analyst

- Cyber vulnerability specialists

- Threat Analyst

- Cybersecurity Threat Analyst

- Cyber Threat Hunter

- Computer Network Defense Analyst

- Cyber Security Incident Response

Being a Professional in the Analyst Category

The daily life of the typical analyst involves staring at a computer screen and consuming data. They work with large data sets and turn them into actionable information. Data will be in the form of individual facts, system logs, statistics, diagrams, and logs from various sources. They take all the data and turn it into reports. For example, a cyber threat hunter could analyze spreadsheets, text documents and websites with the stolen credentials from four hundred soldiers from the army. Perhaps they gathered this data from three different malicious sites on the Dark Web. After analyzing this data, they determine that there are fifteen real usernames on the list and only five of them are still active. The analyst would then create a report that explains what the actual threat was, which users and departments of the organization are affected and how this information was leaked. The analyst has to take time to gather the data, cross reference and check all the accounts, and determine where the threat came from. In this specific example, this would be a cyber threat intelligence or threat hunter type position. You can see why it would be crucial to comprehend IT well enough to be aware of potential exploits and common attacks.

(See attack.mitre.org for a breakdown of the types of attacks that can occur).

The analyst would spend a lot of time searching for information, and coordinating with system administrators who have access to the affected accounts.

Many analysts do shift work in an SOC, but the nature of the work will depend on the requirements of the job. In some positions, there is a need to constantly watch audit logs and identify possible security incidents, report and respond to them in real-time.

Collect and Operate Cybersecurity Category

The "Collect and Operate" category provides specialized denial and deception operations of cybersecurity information that may be used to develop intelligence. Most of the positions in Collect and Operate are for intelligence departments working as contractors for the government. A high level clearance will be needed to allow you to access the information you will be collecting.

In the movie *Mission Impossible: Ghost Protocol*, Jeremy Renner plays a character who calls himself an "Analyst". He would have been in this category of work. In reality these jobs are not as exciting as they are depicted in the movies. Hollywood has these characters jumping off the Burj Khalifa tower in Dubai and fighting bad guys. But in reality, intelligence work is a lot of cubicles and buildings with no windows, sprinkled with some shift work where you have 40 – 50 hours a week of data analysis.

The specialty areas include:

- Collection Operations

- Cyber Operational Planning

- Cyber Operations

Collection Operations

This specialty area includes collecting intelligence from different sources for clients. The work roles, abilities, skills and tasks are for intelligence. This specialty uses different intelligence collection platforms such as systems that search for threats, databases and networks with classified intelligence data from different agencies, and information gathering tools that use artificial intelligence.

Work Roles include:

- All Source-Collection Manager

- All Source-Collection Requirements Manager

Cyber Operational Planning

This area is about Intelligence planning. The roles in this area provide support for developing, coordinating, and overseeing all aspects of the Intelligence centers activities. Work roles provide input throughout all planning functions from translating strategic guidance, through concept and plan development, to plan assessments and associated functions.

Work Roles include:

- Cyber Ops Planner

- Partner Integration Planner

Cyber Operations

Cyber operations gathers evidence on criminal or foreign intelligence entities to mitigate possible or real-time threats, protect against espionage or insider threats, and foreign sabotage and international terrorist. These are the guys in the background researching terrorist cells.

Some work roles include:

- Cyber Operator

- Cyber Analyst

- Cyberspace Intelligence Analyst

- Cyber Defense Operator

The Collect and Operate category consists of mostly intelligence jobs. Although there are degrees that specialize in this category, such as Bachelor of Science program in Cyber Operations, any degree in science, technology, engineering, or mathematics will help. Some of the non-technical Intel analyst positions will even take a degree in Intelligence Studies, Political Science, International Relations, or National Security.

For the more technical cyber analyst positions, see the same certifications that are required in the Analysis security category.

Being a Professional in the Collection and Operations Category

All of these jobs deal with intelligence. They will usually have some affiliation with the federal government. This includes the military, NSA, CIA and other organizations with a direct affiliation with national security. They will usually be operating in a building with no windows, classified phones that encrypt all messages and COMSEC (which we will talk about in another section). They do a lot of coordination with other units within the organization.

Many of these jobs do a lot of what professionals in the "Analyze" category do. There is a lot of overlap with the "All-Sources Analyst" specialty because they are spending a lot of time searching and gathering data from different sources to create reports and presentations for decision makers that need it. The main difference is that the collection and operations professional is focused on highly sensitive information in the Intelligence community.

Investigate Cybersecurity Category

This category of the cybersecurity work force focuses on investigation of crimes that involve the use of information systems, networks, and digital evidence. This part of cybersecurity has been made popular by shows like "CSI" that have cybersecurity forensics in the plot of the show from time to time. In fact, one of the spin offs of the CSI series is called *CSI: Cyber*.

The specialty areas include:

- Cyber Investigation
- Digital Forensics

Cyber Investigation

This specialty area applies tactics, techniques and procedures with a full range of investigative tools. Cyber investigation includes interviews interrogation, surveillance, and surveillance detection.

Work roles include:

- Cyber Crime Investigator
- Digital Forensics Analyst
- Criminal Investigator (Digital Forensics)

The cybercrime investigator and digital forensics specialties overlap. The primary distinction between the two is that a cybercrime investigator focuses more on law enforcement while digital forensics focuses on extracting data from information systems that are involved in crimes.

Digital Forensics

The digital forensics specialty area collects, processes, preserves, analyzes, and presents computer-related evidence in support of network vulnerability mitigation, criminal, fraud, counterintelligence, or law enforcement investigations.

The work roles include:

- Cyber Defense Forensics Analyst
- Law Enforcement / Counterintelligence Forensics Analysts
- Digital Network Exploitation Analyst

Being a Professional in the Investigate Category

The Investigate category requires a combination of experience, degrees or certifications. If you research the types of degrees for this field, you will see that many will accept any science, technical, engineering or math degree if you have experience with digital forensics. If you will be working with law enforcement, a criminal justice degree or a background in law enforcement will help.

Criminal Investigator's and digital forensics' salaries vary greatly because this skill is necessary in almost every industry. According to ZipRecruiter, the majority of digital forensics investigators make between $51K and 110K, with a national average of about $80K per year. But there are so many factors with the investigate category that it will depend on the position itself.

There are some certifications that will help get into this career field. The top certs are listed on the Department of Defense approved list. This includes the GCFA, GIAC Certified Forensic Analyst.

The training is on SANS.org as *FOR508: Advanced Computer Forensic Analysis and Incident Response*. Other DoD approved certifications that are accepted for federal forensics positions include GCIA, GIAC Certified Intrusion Analyst.

There are many other forensics certifications that can help in the field:

- GIAC Certified Forensic Examiner (GCFE)
- GIAC Certified Forensic Analyst (GCFA)
- GIAC Reverse Engineering Malware (GREM)
- GIAC Network Forensic Analyst (GNFA)
- GIAC Advanced Smartphone Forensics (GASF)
- GIAC Cyber Threat Intelligence (GCTI)
- Computer Hacking Forensics Investigator (CHFI)
- Certified Computer Examiner (CCE)
- Cyber Security Forensic Analyst (CSFA)
- EnCase certification

Some of the tools that Digital Forensics professionals are proficient on include:

- Encase
- FTK (Forensics Toolkit)
- The Sleuth Kit
- SIFT
- Xplico
- Tcpdump
- hexadecimal dumper
- disassembler to analyze software
- debugger to analyze software

- Snort

- Zeek

Many of these positions blend in with both network forensics and cyber security analysis. Sometimes their jobs overlap or they work back-to-back in the same office on the same cases.

The daily life of a professional conducting investigative work will vary. With a focus on cybersecurity analyst work, the daily tasks will be monitoring audit logs throughout the agency. The skills of an Intrusion Analyst would come in handy for this. They spend their day doing network forensics which includes doing packet captures using tools like Wireshark, Snort, Tcpdump, SiLK and other tools. If most of their tasks include doing cyber security analyst work, they will only scan hard drives or conduct packet analysis as needed.

When I worked in a security operations center as a cybersecurity analyst, I would have to use Tcpdump and some packet capture tools. We would do a little forensics work, but as soon as it got deep, we would pass it along to our digital forensics team who would spend hours or days on a couple of potential incidents.

For the digital forensic professional working with special investigations of a law enforcement unit, they are given computer components to analyze. They use tools like FTK, EnCase and others to gather data that may be used in an ongoing criminal investigation. These computer components include internal or external hard drives, RAM, and anything that stores data. They will work with detectives, agencies and other law enforcement personnel on cases.

Positions that are heavy on digital forensics look for experience in the field above all else. Tools can be taught and certification tests can be passed, but experience conducting log file analysis is priceless.

Unspeakable Crimes

I have had two run-ins with the criminal investigations side of digital forensics work for law enforcement. Both incidents involved the same crime.

Years ago, when I was working on the Help Desk at an Air Force base, we were fixing a workstation that kept rebooting. Our attempts to remotely resolve the problem were unsuccessful, so we went to the desk of the Master Sergeant that was having the issue.

After booting it successfully in "Safe Mode" we decided that it might be malware. We ran a scan. The scan detected multiple viruses. When we looked at the drive where the malware was located, there was a whole bunch of porn. Pornography on a military system is bad. We would find it from time to time on workstations. It usually was met with a chuckle, a quick evaluation of the quality of said porn and then deletion. But there are some kinds of pornography that would get your system confiscated for further investigation with digital forensics and land the operator of that system in jail, kicked out the military and registered as a sex offender. I'm sure you can figure out what kind of pornography I'm talking about.

When we found the illegal pornography, we started a security incident that was immediately send to the Air Force Office of Special Investigations; it's the CSI of the US Air Force. They investigate domestic and international terrorists, murders and the type of porn that we found on this master sergeant's computer. The office of special investigations confiscated the system, gathered additional Internet logs from the network team and started putting all the data together to investigate the case. The last I heard of that sergeant he was in the process of losing his rank and retiring.

The second time I had a run-in with the criminal investigations side of digital forensics was when I was out of the military. I was on a small security team in an aerospace company. Once again, someone's workstation had some sort of virus on it. The system was running too slow to do work and we could not fix the issue remotely. Someone on our team had to go to the employee's office.

The cybersecurity professional ran a local scan, found the malware and a motherload of illegal pornography. The system was confiscated for further investigation. This guy was close to retirement. I don't know why someone would risk their livelihood by doing this! Especially at work. I mean, they have to know that the network is being monitored and that the organization can scan your system at any time, right?

Anyway, I digress. In digital forensics and law enforcement you really see dark stuff. Do not get into this field if you cannot handle it.

Operate and Maintain Cybersecurity Category

This category covers support, administration, and maintenance necessary to ensure effective and efficient information system performance and security. You will notice that the work roles are mostly information technology positions that include support for cybersecurity tasks rather than full time cybersecurity roles.

Specialty areas include:

- Customer Service and Technical Support

- Data Administration

- Knowledge Management

- Network Services

- System Administration

- System Analysis

Customer Service and Technical Support

Technical support specialist is a work role within the Customer Service and Technical Support specialty area. Technical customer services help customers who need endpoint support for hardware and software.

This specialty area is great for entry level positions. It also includes work roles like help desk, help desk supervisor, field technician, customer support and others.

Being in Customer Service

This work role supports the largest range of experience. What I mean is that it can accept both novices with no experience, and information technology professionals with over ten years of experience.

Since the range of professionals is so broad, the average that technical support specialist make is about $40K USD annually. Of course, there are customer service type positions that make much more than this.

Some entry level customer support positions will accept a beginner with a high school diploma or equivalent. Many companies will give on the job training, but they do expect you to come to the table with some basic IT knowledge.

As for degrees, when they do ask for a degree, they ask for everything from technical Associate's degrees to Master's degrees. It will depend on whether the system is technical, managerial or director level.

Entry level certifications that I recommend include the ones on the DoD approved list such as the CompTIA A+, Security+, ISC2 SSCP and the GSEC. But other entry level certifications that are great are Amazon AWS Cloud Practitioner and the Google IT Support Profession certification. These are marketable entry level certifications. They will not give you 100,000 USD by themselves but they are a good start.

The main tasks of customer support specialists include taking calls, requests, servicing tickets, and troubleshooting end-user devices. End-user devices includes laptops, desk top computers, and mobile devices. On a day-to-day basis they troubleshoot hardware and software issues on local systems. These tasks include doing some security on the systems such as installing security patches, updating malware signatures and ensuring that systems have proper security configurations.

Data Administration

The data administration specialty includes professionals who develop and administer databases. These data management systems allow the storage, query, protection, and utilization of data. The work roles include database administrators and data analysts.

Data Analyst

Data analysts examine data from different sources and provide insight on security and privacy. They design and implement custom algorithms for data mining and research purposes.

Database Administrator

Database administrators (also known as DBAs) have many security base tasks. These include allowing the secure storage, query, protection and utilization of data. This includes security updates and security / privacy configurations.

Being a DBA and Data Analyst

DBAs and Data analysts spend most of their time with large sets of data. The difference is that a DBA is working with the system that manages the data (the relational or object oriented databased and the hardware). They might work with Oracle, MS SQL or other vendor database systems that house the data. They might need to create queries, manage users or update security configurations on the database.

DBAs make an average of 120K USD per year and Data Analysts make an average of 90KUSD. This depends on the level of experience, location and skill set.

The top DBA certifications are:

- Oracle Certified Associate - Oracle9i Database Administrator (OCA)

- Oracle Certified Professional - Oracle 9i Database Administrator (OCP)

- Microsoft Certified Database Administrator (MCDBA)

- Oracle 9i Database Administrator - Professional (OCP)

- Oracle Database 10g Administrator Certified Professional

- SQL Server 2008, Implementation and Maintenance (MCTS)

- Teradata 14 Certified Master

DBA positions rely heavily on experience and skills because there is a lot riding on managing the organization's databases.

A data analyst works with the organization's data. They take statistics, mean averages, sums, income, gross sales, units sold, differences and make that information into graphs, pie charts and other information that will be meaningful to the organization.

Data analyst positions vary but they are usually looking for a combination of the following skills:

- Advanced Microsoft Excel skills

- Pivot Tables, Macros

- Strong communication skills, both written and verbal

- Experience working with Big Data

- Structured Query Language (SQL)

- Machine learning algorithms

- Data visualization/Tableau

- Python and other scripting languages

- Decision-making

- Building data sets

- Machine learning models

- Predictive modeling

- Statistical analysis

- Data engineering

- Regression analysis

- Data optimization

Some of the tools that data analysts use include:

- Microsoft Excel

- Python

- "R" analytics

- Jupyter Notebook (jupyter.org)

- Apache Spark

- SAS

- Microsoft Power B.I.

- Tableau

- KNIME

Data analytics positions are not usually looking for any particular IT certifications. But here are a few of the top data analyst certifications:

- CompTIA Data+

- Microsoft Certified Data Analyst Associate

- Cloudera Certified Associate (CCA) Data Analyst

- SAS Certified Big Data Professional

- Certified Analytics Professional (CAP)

- Amazon AWS Certified Data Analytics

- IBM Data Science Professional Certificate

- Google Data Analytics Professional Certificate

Knowledge Management

The Knowledge Manager position is under the knowledge management specialty, and this person is responsible for administering tools that allow an organization to identify, document, and access its content.

The Knowledge Manager Role

Knowledge manager positions vary in responsibilities based on the industry. In the government, the knowledge manager may need to coordinate with servicemen, civil servants and contractors to develop training and knowledge transfer requirements and policies. A military or Intelligence based knowledge manager may help protect and distribute classified information in the correct way.

In a more technical role, the knowledge manager will be more like DBAs where they provide analysis, design, development, and deployment support for customer database requirements. They may need to know SQL and how to create queries.

The degrees and experience level also vary greatly based on the job and the organization's data requirements.

I have seen organizations take program managers, information system security officers or general managers and make them the official knowledge manager.

Network Services

The Cybersecurity Workforce only mentions the network operator specialist as a work role. A network operator specialist "plans, implements, and operates network services, to include hardware and virtual environments". The full breakdown of network services in the NICE framework is a little out of touch. So, we will address what you really need to know about this specialty area.

First of all, I seldom ever come across the job titles "network operator specialist" in network services. Network engineers and network administrators is what we call them in the IT industry. You have network technicians, network support, and other names but the most popular are engineers and administrators. There are basic skills all network operators need to know for network switches and routers and other internetworking devices. They need to know how to setup a local area network, connect to a wide area network, configure, upgrade, and backup a switch, router or other internetworking devices.

There are different specialties in network operations. Voice over IP (VOIP), network security, virtual networks and others. Network support only does work when something breaks or if there is a change needed on the network. Network operators have these types of skills:

- Network engineering

  o   LAN management

  o   WAN management

- Operational support

- OSI model

- Multicasting knowledge: IPv4 and IPv6

- Virtual networking

Being an Entry-Level Network Associate

The network industry is dominated by a few huge organizations that have a bit of an oligopoly on the IT market. As such, if you are a network engineer you will need to eventually know at least one vendor's products and services well.

The major companies providing professional network enterprise services are:

- Cisco

- Juniper Networks

- NVIDIA

- VMware

- Hewlett Packard Enterprise (Aruba Networks)

- Riverbed Technology

- Extreme Networks

- NetScout

The organizations that have the best products and services for an IT professional to know are Cisco, VMware and Juniper.

Unfortunately, because their products and services are continuously changing, their certificates also do. The following breakdown of vendor certifications may have changed by the time you read this.

For Cisco, the entry level certification is called CCT (Cisco Certified Technician). At the time of this writing, it is the only entry-level Cisco cert below the CCNA (Cisco Certified Network Associate) which is an intermediate certification.

Another Entry level network certification is the CompTIA Network+. Although not many organizations are looking for this certification, it will give you a good idea of the basics of networks.

Juniper Networks Certified Associate, or Junos (JNCIA-Junos), is the associate-level certification for Juniper Networks technologies. It covers the fundamentals of networking using Juniper systems.

VMware's certification path starts with the VMware Certified Technical Associate (VCTA). This certification is for entry-level operators new to the industry of virtualized environments.

Each of the industry leaders in network enterprise solutions have their own training and certifications. The entry level certifications don't have as much marketability but they are great for learning and getting your foot in the door.

Intermediate network engineers

The intermediate networking level is where the money is made. These are certifications that are highly sought after by many employers around the world. These include:

- Cisco Certified Network Associate (CCNA)
- Juniper Networks enterprise routing and switching platforms (JNCIS-ENT)
- VMware Certified Professional

The job of an intermediate network engineer is to install, configure, and troubleshoot networks using products from one of the major networking service providers. The intermediate certification will allow an associate to work as a technician in one or more areas, including routing and switching, security, wireless services, or data center operations. While specifics of the job vary, the responsibilities may involve evaluating network performance, defining policies and procedures, and improving network security. Some of the necessary skills include:

- Network engineering
- Routing protocols: EIGRP, OSPF, BGP
- Operational support
- SAN networking knowledge
- Unified Communication
- OSI model
- Multicasting knowledge: IPv4 and IPv6
- Firewalls
- Virtual networking

Professional Level Network Engineers

A network engineer at the professional level is responsible for maintaining, implementing, and resolving technical issues relating to local and wide area networks at the enterprise level using the applicable network device. They have the skills to collaborate with specialists in cybersecurity, Voice over IP, wireless, and video solutions. The need to be able to activate and manage routing protocols such as EIGRP and OSPF that are necessary for getting wide area networks to communicate.

Network professionals can design and develop Layer 3 Path Control Solutions and broadband connections as well as VLAN based solutions for an enterprise. The certifications include (but are not limited to):

- Cisco Certified Network Professional (CCNP)

- VMware Certified Professional (VCP)

- Enterprise Routing and Switching, Professional (JNCIP-ENT)

Systems Administrator

System Admins are the first work role that come to mind when people think about "operate and maintain". There are system admins for every type of system from desktops to servers to firewalls.

Excluding network and database administrators, most system admins are either Red Hat or Microsoft professionals. Truthfully, the term "system administrator" can cover just about anything from firewalls to mainframes to web servers. Regardless of the technology, they are doing operational management of the system.

These days, most companies require certifications of their system administrators to ensure that their employees are not falling behind. There are exceptions. Some organizations don't care about certifications or degrees, but in these cases, they lean heavily on proven skills and knowledge level. According to the US Bureau of Labor Statistics, systems administrator roles are projected to grow 4 percent from 2019 to 2029.

Here are some common requirements that you would find in a system administrator job description:

- Install and configure software, hardware and networks

- Ensure security and efficiency of IT infrastructure

- Monitor system performance and troubleshoot issues

- Identify system requirements and install upgrades

- Maintains, secure and upgrade a web system

- Create a backup and safeguard the data

- Perform account setup for new and old employees

- Track emerging technologies and implement them in the organization

Some of the most marketable certifications include:

- Microsoft Certified Solutions Expert (MCSE)

- VMware Certified Professional (VCP)

- Oracle Linux System Administrator (Oracle)

- ITIL® Certification

- Red Hat Certified Engineer (RHCE)

This list changes with the trends of the market.

Oversee and Govern Cybersecurity Category

This category provides leadership, management, guidance and advocacy so the organization may effectively conduct cybersecurity work. This is one of the most important categories that doesn't get the attention it deserves. It includes security compliance, governance, C-Level executives, program management and training.

The specialty areas include:

- Cybersecurity Management
- Executive Cyber Leadership
- Legal Advice and Advocacy
- Program/Project Management and Acquisition
- Strategic Planning and Policy
- Training, Education, and Awareness

Cybersecurity Management

Cybersecurity management is a specialty area that oversees the cybersecurity program of an information system or network. This category focuses on managing the risks that an information system has and how it will impact the organization as a whole. This includes strategic, personnel, infrastructure, requirements, policy enforcement, and resources.

Work roles mentioned in the cybersecurity workforce framework include:

- Communications Security (COMSEC) Manager

- Information System Security Manager (ISSM)

Communications Security (COMSEC)

The COMSEC officer is the key custodian of Crypto Keys. This is sometimes known as a Crypto Key Management System (CKMS). A COMSEC officer needs to have knowledge of computers and networking concepts such as network security methods. They need to have some understanding of the laws and security policies that govern the COMSEC process as well as knowledge of cryptography. COMSEC is done by other security positions such as Facility Security Officers and Information Systems and Security Manager (ISSM).

If you research the work roles in the market, you will see this job given to Information System Security Officers, Program Security Officers, Contract Special Security Officers (CSSO), Contract Special Security Officers, and System Security Engineer positions. These are highly classified jobs working with military departments and the Intelligence Community.

Employers of COMSEC officers are looking for Active Top Secret clearances. They are looking for someone who has experience interpreting and enforcing government and company security policies, and providing direction.

Information System Security Manager (ISSM)

An ISSM is responsible for cybersecurity of a program, organization, system or enclaves. The ISSM manages the Information System Security Officer (ISSO). Information system security covers part of governance, risk and compliance (GRC), because their main focus is on security compliance. All major industries have to comply with governing country, state and industry rules and regulations.

For example, in the USA, the healthcare industry must comply with Health Insurance Portability and Accountability Act of 1996 (HIPAA). The financial industry must follow the rules of the Sarbanes Oxley Act (SOX). SOX requires all financial reports to include an Internal Controls Report. The US government requires all federal information systems to abide by the Federal Information Security Modernization Act (FISMA) which has NIST special publication 800 guidance. Each industry in each country and state has different rules and regulations they must abide by and the ISSM is a role that assists with this.

Being an Information System Security Professional Jobs

ISSM specifically is a management role over information system security professionals. Information System Security professionals cover a large part of security compliance. There is a wide range of job titles for them in the US federal government:

- Compliance officers

- Risk Compliance

- Information System Security Officers

- Cyber Security Engineer

- Senior Information System Security Officer

In the healthcare industry they have a different set of titles:

- Compliance Analyst

- Privacy Compliance

- Risk Analyst Health Information

- IS Security GRC Analyst

- Chief Compliance Officer

- Senior Cybersecurity Risk Analyst

- Compliance officer

In the financial sector, the names are as follows:

- Cybersecurity Senior Analyst

- Information Security Risk and Compliance Analyst

- Senior Analyst, Internal Controls – IT SOX

- SOX Consultant

- Information Security Governance Analyst

Regardless of the industry, what all these information system security positions and titles have in common is that they all focus on managing the organization's adherence to the industry compliance and help to manage the organization's risk.

Government information security positions lean heavily toward years of experience in IT, but that experience can be leveraged with a degree in STEM (science, technology, engineering or mathematics) or a relevant IT certification.

A CISSP, Security+ or security certification, a BS degree and some IT experience are excellent qualifications for employment in this field with the government doing compliance. But this varies from place to place so make sure you check the requirements of the organization. A solid understanding of ISO 27000, GDPR, NIST, IEC62443 or any security compliance framework is a great way to get in.

A good way to learn more about GRC work is to pursue certifications that focus on this.

> **ISC2 Certified Governance, Risk and Compliance (CGRC)** – This certification is formerly known as the Certified Authorization Professional (CAP). The CGRC focuses on the US federal security compliance which comes from the Federal

Information Security Modernization Act of 2014 and other federal regulations. These federal laws promote the need for security controls, assessments, continuous monitoring and risk management framework. The guidance for this process is in National Institute of Standards and Technology special publications, NIST 800-37, 800-30, 800-53, FIPS 200 and other documents. The domains of the CGRC are information security risk management program, the scope of the information system, selection and approval of security and privacy controls and implementation of security and privacy controls.

ISCA Certified Information Systems Auditor (CISA) - CISA certification for those who audit, control, monitor and assess an organization's information technology and business systems. If you are an entry-level to mid-career professional, CISA can showcase your expertise and assert your ability to apply a risk-based approach to planning, executing and reporting on audit engagements.

ISACA Certified in Risk and Information Systems Control (CRISC) - CRISC focuses on enterprise IT risk management. The domains of this certification are governance, IT risk assessment, risk response and reporting, and IT and security.

ISACA Certified in the Governance of Enterprise IT (CGEIT) – The CGEIT is agnostic. It does not focus on any one framework. This certification covers handling the governance of an entire organization. The domains consist of governance of enterprise IT, IT resources, befits realization and risk optimization.

There are other GRC certifications, but these are the ones with the most marketability at the time of this writing.

Executive Cyber Leadership

These are C-Level executive positions that perform cyber security functions. Examples would be director and chief positions such as chief information officer, chief security officer and others. They are leaders that make decisions that affect the overall direction of the organization and how resources are allocated.

C-Level executives usually hold a master's degree in their trade with a decade or more of experience. I used to think that all C-Level execs were privileged political types that just knew the right people to be given that position... I was wrong.

If you take a look at an executive or director's resume you will usually find something out of the ordinary in their past. They ran (or created) successful organizations, they were brilliant at a prestigious university, they were a high-level officer in the military, they worked at the organization for 20+ years or they started at a low position and climbed the corporate ladder. There will usually be something exceptional about them regardless of any advantages they might have had to get their position.

Chief Information Security Officers

Chief Information Security Officers and Directors of Security tend to be very talented technical experts. In my experience they usually have an incredible depth of technical knowledge on more than one thing. They will sometimes have some combination of a ridiculous number of certifications, a long history in IT, or a graduate degree. The most impressive executives specializing is security are also good at leading.

Once you get to this level, you will need to have your technical skills take a back seat because your job is to lead, provide resources and push the organization to the next level.

Legal Advice and Advocacy

As information processing, storage and transmission has become the center piece of our lives, it makes sense that the legal ramifications of that information must be considered. This specialty provides legal guidance on policy that the organizations sets forth. Work roles include:

- Cyber Legal Advisor

- Privacy Officer / Privacy Compliance Manager

Cyber Legal Advisor

This work role provides legal advice and recommendations on cyber law. Some other related titles include Cyber Claim Counsel, legal counsel, compliance counsel, cyber security associate, and cyber / data / privacy attorney.

The path of this work role requires legal experience. Often, cyber legal advisors are lawyers or paralegals. The cyber legal advisor is expected to have knowledge of data breaches and privacy laws (HIPAA, GLBA, FERPA, CCPA, GDPR, etc.). For cyber claim counsels, the expectation is that there is experience with handling claims.

Responsibilities might include:

- Incident response for cybersecurity and data privacy incidents

- Analysis of state, federal, and international privacy laws

- Drafting legal notices of a data breach to individuals and regulators

- Responding to regulatory investigations arising out of a data breach

- Defending privacy lawsuits

- Drafting privacy and security policies and procedures pursuant to HIPAA, GLBA, CCPA, and other statutes

Certifications that might help this position:

- Certified Paralegal (CP) or Certified Legal Assistant (CLA)

- CORE Registered Paralegal (CRP) or PACE Registered Paralegal (RP)

- American Alliance Certified Paralegal (AACP)

- Advanced Paralegal Certification (APC)

- Professional Paralegal (PP)

Other relevant requirements that you will see for this position includes (but is not limited to):

- A Bachelor's Degree

- Properly licensed, registered or authorized, and in good standing to practice law in the jurisdiction in which you will be working

- Multiple years of relevant legal experience

- J.D. (Juris Doctorate Degree) from an ABA accredited law school

- Licensed or eligible to practice in the applicable state

- Ability to effectively communicate, both written and oral, with the intended audience

- Ability to exercise sound judgment in a fast-paced environment

- Ability to exercise agility and adaptability in providing legal advice

Privacy Officer / Privacy Compliance Manager

Privacy Officers oversee privacy compliance programs of the organization. They are available to provide expertise on governance and policy as well as incident response where privacy is a factor. They might conduct privacy assessments or create privacy documents.

Some other names of this position are:

- Compliance Officer

- Risk and Privacy Officer

- Cybersecurity Officer

- Data Privacy Officer

- Data Privacy specialist

- Privacy - Legal and Compliance Specialist

- Privacy Specialist

Certifications that might help a privacy officer:

- **CIPP (Certified Information Privacy Professional) -** This certification applies to both the U.S. (CIPP/US) and Europe (CIPP/E) law and regulation.

- **CIPM (Certified Information Privacy Manager -** The CIPM covers implementing privacy in an organization.

- **CIPT (Certified Information Privacy Technologist) -** It covers implementing privacy in applications and systems.

- **CDPSE (Certified Data Privacy Solutions Engineer) -** CDPSE is for IT professionals who work with technology and then store, collect and transport personally identifiable information.

Program/Project Management and Acquisition

Applies knowledge of data, information, processes, organizational interactions, skills, and analytical expertise, as well as systems, networks, and information exchange capabilities to manage acquisition programs. Executes duties governing hardware, software, and information system acquisition programs and other program management policies. Provides direct support for acquisitions that use information technology (IT) (including National Security Systems), applying IT-related laws and policies, and provides IT-related guidance throughout the total acquisition life cycle.

IT Investment / Portfolio Manager

This position manages a portfolio of IT investments that align with the overall mission and enterprise priorities. Portfolio managers are investment decision-makers. They construct and manage portfolios, choose what and when to acquire and sell investments, and devise and implement investment strategies and processes to suit client goals and constraints.

Program managers / Project Managers

Here is a little more about program and project management as a work role. Project managers are a crucial part of medium and large system and software engineering projects. They provide scheduling for the development of old and new systems.

If you don't want to be technical, project management is one of the best career paths you could do because there are a lot of positions for this that are aligned closely with cybersecurity, science, software and engineering projects. Many of these positions have remuneration that are comparable to their technical counterparts.

Project Management Professional (PMP)

This means skilled project managers are in high demand. The PMP certification is designed by project professionals, for project professionals and validates that you are among the best—highly skilled in:

- **People:** emphasizing the soft skills you need to effectively lead a project team in today's changing environment.

- **Process:** reinforcing the technical aspects of successfully managing projects.

- **Business Environment:** highlighting the connection between projects and organizational strategy.

PMP certification validates that you have the project leadership skills employers seek. The new PMP includes three key approaches:

- **Predictive** (waterfall)
- **Agile**
- **Hybrid**

Protect & Detect Cybersecurity Category

This category is for all cybersecurity professionals who identify, analyze and mitigate threats to internal information systems and networks. There is some overlap with the Analyze, Investigate and Operate, and Maintain categories because Protecting and Detecting requires skills from each one of these. The difference is that this category is taking action to do something about the threats.

Protect & Detect includes the following specialty areas:

- Cyber Defense Analysis
- Cyber Defense Infrastructure Support
- Incident Response
- Vulnerability Assessment and Management

Cyber Defense Analysis

According to the Cybersecurity and Infrastructure Security Agency (CISA), cyber defense analysis, "Uses defensive measures and information collected from a variety of sources to identify, analyze, and report events that occur or might occur within the network to protect information, information systems, and networks from threats."

The work role that cisa.gov mentions is "Cyber Defense Analyst", but in the cybersecurity field there are many titles for this role. There is information security analyst, cybersecurity analyst, cybersecurity vulnerability analyst and many others. There is even a position in the

National Security Agency for this role called "Forensic Analyst". The role title sounds more like it should be a part of the "Investigate" category. But don't get too wrapped up in the titles of the roles. Since the organization determines what the tasks, knowledge base and title of the role is, the names of the positions will vary. But the work consists of using data collected from intrusion detection systems, firewalls, network traffic logs and other cyber defense tools to mitigate risk.

There is a lot of overlap between this work role and the Analyst cybersecurity category, but the difference is that cyber defense collects this information to actively fix the problem.

When I was doing cybersecurity analyst work for the DoD, I can tell you that there is really not that much difference because the organization might have you shutting down ports with an intrusion prevention one day and doing nothing but analyzing network traffic the next.

Cyber Defense Infrastructure Support

Cyber defense infrastructure support is closely related to cyber defense analyst. The difference is that they focus on making sure that the analyst has the tools to do their job effectively.

When I was in the SOC working with the DoD, I transferred from doing analyst work monitoring the traffic in shifts and correlating data using a security information event manager (SIEM) to supporting the SIEM. I was installing new SIEM hardware, creating reports, queries and dashboards for the cyber analysts.

The work tempo and mindset changed because I went from an all-seeing eye of the network—always watching the network in shifts with my fellow analysts—to someone in more of an "operate and maintain" stance. We would respond if something was broken and we'd be working to update patches but this did not have to be done in a shift.

For Cyber Defense Infrastructure, you will need to know the hardware, software and configurations of the cybersecurity tools.

Being a Cyber Defense Analyst

The government and contracting organizations look for a combination of STEM BS degrees, cybersecurity experience, and cybersecurity certifications. It is also important to have a good understanding of incident response.

Incident Response

An "incident" refers to something that will damage the organization, the asset, the data or the flow of data on a system. These can be malware, a hack, a leak or a mishap. As a cybersecurity analyst, we were part of the incident response team. As such, we were part of the incident response process. This process takes on a few different shapes but we will address the 6-step process that is used by the US government:

1. Preparation: plan ahead before a security incident.

2. Identification: detect and determine what kind of incident (if any).

3. Containment: limit the impact of the incident.

4. Eradication: remove the threat causing the incident.

5. Recovery: restore the affected system or information.

6. Lessons Learned: investigate the root cause.

As cyber defense analysts, we were mostly part of the identification, containment and eradication section of the incident response team. There were incident handlers whose main job was to follow the organization's response from preparation to lessons learned throughout the entire process. There are many names for professional incident handlers:

- Incident Response Analysts

- Technical Security Investigators

- Incident Commander
- Incident Responder
- Incident Response Lead

The names of the positions are irrelevant because there are many positions that will have a hand in incident response tasks. So, their title might be Information Security Associate, Digital Forensics Incident Responder, Security Engineer, Cybersecurity Analyst, Information System Security Officer, or whatever.

Vulnerability Assessment and Management

Vulnerability management is important within an organization's security process. Vulnerabilities are constantly being discovered on all operating systems, applications, hardware, and firmware. Sometimes the vendor catches them and announces a patch or configuration that must be implemented to remediate the risk. And sometimes hackers discover weaknesses in the system. The organization must be proactive in conducting regular vulnerability assessments to have strong cyber defenses. The workload is so heavy in medium and large environments that companies and government departments usually have an office dedicated solely to vulnerability management.

Tips on Cyber Defense Analysis Positions

All Cyber Defense Analysis positions have the same types of certifications that employers like to see. The top paying cybersecurity certifications that are marketable for this field are:

- CISSP
- CISA
- CEH
- GCIA
- GCIH
- Security+
- CYSA+
- GPEN

There are others but these will be the most popular because they are listed on the DoD approved certification list. These are listed in Appendix A under Cybersecurity Service Provider Analyst and Cybersecurity Services Provider Infrastructure Support and Cybersecurity Services Provider Incident Handler.

Securely Provision Cybersecurity Category

This category provides concepts, designs, procedures and building secure information systems and networks. The focus is on making sure that security controls are being put in place as systems are being developed.

The specialty areas are:

- Risk Management

- Software Development

- System Architecture

- System Development

- Systems Requirements Planning

- Technology R&D

- Test and Evaluation

Risk Management

This specialty area is responsible for overseeing, evaluating and supporting the documentation, validation, assessment and authorization process required to ensure that new and existing systems meet risk requirements.

The Information System Security Manager (ISSM) and team will do a lot of the documentation and assist with assessments for the authorization process, but this specialty is focused on overseeing the final product. This is done by the Authorizing Official and the Security Control Assessor roles.

Authorizing Official / Designating Representative

These are upper-level managers, senior officials, C-Level executives or high-level officers. The organization gives them authority to formally assume responsibility for the secure operations of an information system at an acceptable level of risk.

The reason why this position is important is that having a high-level person sign on behalf of the organization ensures that there will be a serious level of scrutiny when considering the protection of the organization's assets, individuals and even the nation. CIO, CISOs, commanders, and directors are often tasked with being the Authorizing Official for a given system. In my experience, the AO is more of a duty than a permanent position.

Security Control Assessor (SCA)

SCAs conduct comprehensive assessments of all the security controls implemented on a system. This includes the technical, management, operational, physical and environmental controls of an information system. Organizations depend on SCA's to conduct independent, impartial assessments to determine if the controls have been implemented effectively. The SCA gathers the requirements of the organization. They create a security assessment plan that specifies what will be assessed, the scope of the assessment, who will be needed as a point of contact, the timing, and the location of the assessment. When they conduct the assessment, they conduct interviews, test security components and observe the security features and documentation. The results of the assessment are put into a security assessment report and delivered to the leadership of the organization.

Since SCA teams need all types of skillsets, the experience levels and certifications will vary. The tools and techniques they use might include:

- Network / vulnerability scanners

- Compliance scanners

- Code analysis tools

- Web scanners

- Policy, process and procedures reviews

- Wireless assessments

- Penetration testing

- Phishing campaign

- Social Engineering

- Physical security checks

- Cloud security assessment

All of this depends on the organization's requirements and the type of assessment being conducted.

Software Development

Software development must include methods to secure the code being developed. Software developers should follow a software development life cycle (SDLC). Software development life cycle is a process of planning, Analysis, Design, Implementation, Testing and Integration and Maintenance. The SDLC creates, tests and deploys information systems across hardware and software. During the SDLC process the organization is supposed to have security in mind from the beginning of the process. A project manager is a huge help in the software development process.

There are various SDLC methods including:

Waterfall – a linear model that has the software development go in steps. The next step cannot start until the last one is complete.

Agile – this process relies on user input and experience from the old application, to make the new software better. This allows more responsive feedback for better software releases.

Iterative – a process that focuses on baby steps. Making small improvements where needed on the software.

DevOps – similar to Agile, it focuses on usability, gathering user feedback and making improvements. This is done during design and implementation phases.

Spiral – uses a combination of iterative SDLC method and sequential to allow incremental release of software.

Cybersecurity workforce points out two work roles in the software development specialty area: Secure Software Assessor and Software Developer.

Software Engineers

Security is very important in software engineering even though it is sometimes regarded as an afterthought.

Currently, the most in-demand programming languages are JavaScript, Python, HTML, CSS, Java, SQL, NoSQL, C#, Rust, Perl, Go, PHP.

1. JavaScript

JavaScript is responsible for making the websites you go to more responsive. When you hover over a menu it seems to pop off the pages or change colors. This is usually JavaScript code making this happen. Some of what you see in search engines, social media, phone apps and ecommerce is not possible without JavaScript. It is currently the most used client-side scripting language. Things like autocomplete, validation of web form input, loading content to a page without reloading the page, animated page elements and many other things are possible because of JavaScript.

What this language is usually used for:

- Web development
- Game development
- Mobile apps
- Building web servers

2. Python

Python is one of the top languages for cybersecurity professionals to use. It can automate tasks across the cyberattack life cycle for both cyber attackers and defenders. It's used for malware analysis, decoding packets, network scans, server access and much more. Data scientists also use it for visualizing data.

What this language is used for:

- Backend development

- Automating tasks

- Data science

- App development

3. HTML

Hypertext Markup Language is the language that needs no introduction. It is used for website development, web documents, and website maintenance.

4. CSS

Cascading Style Sheets (CSS) is a style sheet language used for describing the presentation of a document written in a markup language such as HTML.

5. Java

Java is a class-based, object-oriented programming language that is designed to have as few implementation dependencies as possible. As such, it is used for just about everything. It can be used to make applications for almost every platform from supercomputers to web sites. It is used in every industry.

6. SQL

Structured Query Language is a language for databases. It is used to communicate with databases in order to manage, sort and filter data. SQL is commonly used for:

- Database management
- Sales reports
- Business management

7. NoSQL

Unlike Structured Query Language, NoSQL is used for different database management models besides traditional relational databases including document, columnar and graph formats.

8. C# / C++

C# and C++ are programming languages that are used for operating systems, applications, games, data structure and many other things. These languages are commonly used in:

- Game development
- Desktop/web/mobile apps
- VR

9. Rust

Rust is a low-level programming language. This means that it is used to communicate directly with hardware and memory. It is used for:

- Operating systems
- VR
- Web browsers

10. Perl

Like Python, Perl is often used for backend server automation. It is used by system administrators for network programming and graphic user interface development. It is a great language to learn for cybersecurity professionals to process log files or grab data.

11. Go

Go is a language that is used for system and network programming, audio/video editing, and Big Data.

12. PHP

PHP is used for server side scripting, managing dynamic content, and is compatible with all operating systems.

Regardless of the language, software needs to be developed with security in mind.

Secure Software Assessor

The work role Secure Software Assessor has many different names including Security Control Assessor, Application Security Engineer (AppSec), Cyber Security Third Party Assessor, and Information Security Risk Assessment Analyst.

Their job is to analyze the security of new or existing computer applications, software, or specialized utility programs, and provide actionable results.

Secure Software Assessors are expected to have an understanding of security best practices and experience with one or more programming languages. A deep understanding of cybersecurity frameworks and standards will sometimes be expected with certain organizations. Cybersecurity frameworks and laws include: PCI, HIPAA, Data Privacy, NIST 800, or ISO 27001/27002.

Some employers are looking for experience in software analysis tools that provide Static Application Security Testing (SAST), Dynamic Analysis Security Testing (DAST), Software Composition Analysis (SCA), Interactive Application Security Test (IAST), Runtime Application Self Protection (RASP), and threat modeling.

System Architecture

If you look up a system architect you will find position titles like Cybersecurity Engineer, System Security Engineer and many others. The System Architecture specialist area is about developing and maintaining business, system, and information processes to support enterprise mission needs. This specialty also develops information technology rules and requirements that describe baseline and target architectures.

Enterprise and Security Architects

Information Technology security architects ensure that all individuals involved with the development of the system follow the rules and requirements that describe the baseline.

The Enterprise Architects supports the design and implementation of the system's architecture. They are part of the development effort. They provide technical expertise in creating, updating, and maintaining architecture data as related to the organization's architectural framework.

The Enterprise Architecture will have deep understanding of technical architectures, putting networks and information systems together. They might have a background in implementing solutions in a cloud environment and making it compliant with NIST security or other security frameworks.

Security Architects ensure that the stakeholder security requirements necessary to protect the organization's mission and business process are in place.

System Development

The System Development Specialty Area focuses on the development phases of the systems development life cycle. It is important that the security features are considered during the system development life cycle (SDLC) of a system. Many organizations will attempt to put security into a system after it is already in production. This is both risky and expensive. It is risky because they don't know the potential weaknesses exposed in a production environment where the system is storing, processing or transferring mission essential data. It is expensive because it is much harder to put the security features in after it has already been designed, installed or implemented.

The System Development Specialty Area has two work roles that develop the system: Information Systems Security Developer & Systems Developer. Adhering to the SDLC is a normal part of any cybersecurity job that involves the development of the system.

Systems Requirements Planning

The Systems Requirements Planning consults with customers to gather and evaluate functional requirements and translates them into technical solutions. In some cases, they assist with development and maintenance of the program protection plan & cybersecurity strategy.

Every time I have encountered them, they have represented the organization and worked with the program manager and other subject matter experts to make sure the system requirements are being met.

DoD Approved Baseline Certifications has a focus on system security architecture. These are listed under the Information Assurance System Architect and Engineer (IASAE). The suggested certifications include:

- CompTIA CASP+ CE

- ISC2 CISSP (or Associate)

- ISC2 CSSLP

- ISC2 CISSP-ISSAP

- ISC2 CISSP-ISSEP

- ISC2 CCSP

Technology and Testing

The last two Specialty Areas of the Securely Provision category are Technology R&D and Test and Evaluate. Technology R&D is for research and Development. R&D conducts technology assessments and integration processes. They support prototypes in testing environments and evaluate their utility.

Test and Evaluations, sometimes called T&E, develop tests to evaluate compliance with organizational requirements. They also conduct the tests. They verify and validate whether the system is functional for operators and performs satisfactorily.

I have worked closely with T&E as a cybersecurity professional. We would have a new mission critical system that was a prototype. I was there to make sure that the security controls were in place and the verification and validation team (T&E) was there to make sure the system worked properly. We called this team verification and validation, but their official title was Systems Engineering. Their main job was to ensure that all government requirements were met on the system. They had comprehensive technical drawings of every single component of the system. They had technical writers, requirements people and a manager.

Most of the requirements people had BS or MS degrees in STEM, a technical background in either computers or engineering, and had to know a lot about how the system's main components worked.

Cybersecurity Scientists & Mathematicians

I have worked for a couple of agencies that had scientists. Many times they would have issues with applying security controls. Sometimes they needed special systems with custom security features. Some security controls would make their job harder or interfere with their research. They didn't understand why any security features needed to be implemented if they were the only person touching the system.

With all the recent leaks of sensitive information and multimillion dollar breaches, everyone has a better understanding of why cybersecurity is so important.

Engineers, analysts and technicians get a lot of the spotlight. These work roles are all over the Cybersecurity Workforce Framework. But you won't find too many scientists and mathematicians covered in the framework.

These two areas are foundational to a lot of the most important work currently being done in cybersecurity. Compilers and programming languages, cryptography, networking protocols, and central processing units (just to name a few) are based on mathematics and science.

Cybersecurity Scientist

Engineers and scientists are often used interchangeably but the two roles have different goals. A scientist in IT is usually discovering, analyzing, testing or developing something new that is not yet intended for commercial use. Engineers in IT are often working with commercial components to develop, analyze, or fix a solution that is within the requirements of an organization. Despite certain similarities, there are many differences between them. Engineers work on practical, operational systems that are already in production, whereas scientists frequently work in a lab on theoretical systems that may never make it to a real-world environment.

Scientists will have doctorates and master's degrees and be very deep in one area or another. At this level, IT certifications are irrelevant because their level of knowledge and degrees have eclipsed any certification they might have. But there are exceptions.

Here are some examples of actual job titles that a cybersecurity scientist might have:

- Research Analysts & Post Doctorate

- Cyber-crime scientist

- Data Scientist - Cybersecurity

- Research Scientist

- Laboratory Scientist

- Research Data Scientist

- Computational Scientist

- Cybersecurity Data Scientist

- Cybersecurity Computer Scientist

- Threat Data Scientist

- Professor

Cryptographers / Mathematicians

I used to think that most mathematicians worked as teachers or professors at a university writing on large chalkboards. I didn't see much practical use for advanced mathematics in everyday life. I was wrong.

Many people are familiar with mathematicians in academia, but mathematicians also work in many other fields, including:

- Astronomy and space exploration

- Climate study

- Medicine

- National security

- Robotics

- Animated films

According to the Department of Labor, the top employers of mathematicians and statisticians are the federal government, and scientific research and development companies. Mathematicians and statisticians may work on teams with engineers, scientists, and other specialists.

Mathematicians held about 2,000 jobs in 2021. The largest employers of mathematicians were as follows:

Federal government – 62%

Professional, scientific, and technical services – 13%

Colleges, universities, and professional schools; state, local, and private – 13%

Statisticians held about 34,200 jobs in 2021. The largest employers of statisticians were as follows:

Federal government – 15%

Research and development in the physical, engineering, and life sciences – 14%

Colleges, universities, and professional schools; state, local, and private – 9%

Healthcare and social assistance – 8%

Insurance carriers and related activities – 6%

Many of the mathematicians working in the federal government are doing cryptography. Cryptography is the study of secure communication techniques that allow only the sender and intended recipient of a message to view its contents.

Within government agencies like the FBI and NSA, there are self-contained training programs for cryptanalysts that take them from complete novices to experts, usually in about three years.

Given the three-year time frame for comprehensive training, it's clear that cryptanalysis is a highly-involved, demanding, and technical skill.

Fortunately for cryptanalysts, there are several trade associations available.

- International Association of Cryptologic Research (IACR)

- International Financial Cryptography Association (IFCA)

- American Crypto Association-ACA

Appendix A: DoD Approved Certifications

Cybersecurity Jobs & Career Paths

Information Assurance Technician (IAT) Level I	Information Assurance Technician (IAT) Level II	Information Assurance Technician (IAT) Level III
A+ CE CCNA-Security CND Network+ CE SSCP	CCNA Security CySA+ GICSP GSEC Security+ CE CND SSCP	CASP+ CE CCNP Security CISA CISSP (or Associate) GCED GCIH CCSP
Information Assurance Manager (IAM) Level I	**Information Assurance Manager (IAM) Level II**	**Information Assurance Manager (IAM) Level III**
CAP CND Cloud+ GSLC Security+ CE HCISPP	CAP CASP+ CE CISM CISSP (or Associate) GSLC CCISO HCISPP	CISM CISSP (or Associate) GSLC CCISO
Information Assurance Architect and Engineer (IASAE) I	**Information Assurance Architect and Engineer (IASAE) II**	**Information Assurance Architect and Engineer (IASAE) III**
CASP+ CE CISSP (or Associate) CSSLP	CASP+ CE CISSP (or Associate) CSSLP	CISSP-ISSAP CISSP-ISSEP CCSP
Cybersecurity Service Provider (CSSP) Analyst	**Cybersecurity Service Provider (CSSP) Infrastructure Support**	**Cybersecurity Service Provider (CSSP) Incident Responder**
CEH CFR CCNA Cyber Ops CCNA-Security CySA+ GCIA GCIH GICSP Cloud+ SCYBER PenTest+	CEH CySA+ GICSP SSCP CHFI CFR Cloud+ CND	CEH CFR CCNA Cyber Ops CCNA-Security CHFI CySA+ GCFA GCIH SCYBER PenTest+
Cybersecurity Service Provider (CSSP) Auditor	**Cybersecurity Service Provider (CSSP) Manager**	
CEH CySA+ CISA GSNA CFR PenTest	CISM CISSP-ISSMP CCISO	

Certification Provider	Certification Name
CertNexus	CyberSec First Responder (CFR)
Cisco	Cisco Certified Network Associate-Security (CCNA-Security)
	Cisco Certified Network Professional-Security (CCNP-Security)
	Cybersecurity Specialty Certification (SCYBER)
Computing Technology Industry Association (CompTIA)	A+ Continuing Education (CE); Cloud Plus (Cloud+)
	Security+ Continuing Education (CE)
	CompTIA Advanced Security Practitioner (CASP) Continuing Education (CE)
	Network+ Continuing Education (CE); Cybersecurity Analyst (CySA+ **)
	PenTest+
EC-Council	Certified Ethical Hacker (CEH); Certified Chief Information Security Officer (CCISO)
	Computer Hacking Forensics Investigator (CHFI); Certified Network Defender (CND)
International Information Systems Security Certifications Consortium (ISC)2	Certified Information Systems Security Professional (CISSP) (or Associate - this means the individual has qualified for the certification except for the number of years experience)
	Certified Secure Software Lifecycle Professional (CSSLP)
	Certification Authorization Professional (CAP)
	Information Systems Security Architecture Professional (ISSAP)
	Information Systems Security Engineering Professional (ISSEP)
	Information Systems Security Management Professional (ISSMP)
	System Security Certified Practitioner (SSCP); Certified Cloud Security Professional (CCSP)
	Health Care Information Security and Privacy Practitioner (HCISPP)
Information Systems Audit and Control Association (ISACA)	Certified Information Systems Auditor (CISA); Certified Information Security Manager (CISM)
Global Information Assurance Certification (GIAC)	GIAC Certified Enterprise Defender (GCED); GIAC Certified Forensic Analyst (GCFA)
	GIAC Certified Incident Handler (GCIH); GIAC Certified Intrusion Analyst (GCIA)
	GIAC Global Industrial Cyber Security Professional (GICSP)
	GIAC Security Essentials Certification (GSEC); GIAC Security Leadership Certificate (GSLC)
	GIAC Systems and Network Auditor (GSNA)
Logical Operations, Inc.	CyberSec First Responder (CFR)

Cybersecurity Jobs

Work from Home

Book 4

Find Cybersecurity Jobs

By

Bruce Brown, CISSP, ISC2 CAP

I love working from home!

I have been working from home since 2014, and it's been great!

For me, "working from home" is not about literally working from my house but about having the freedom to work from anywhere.

I have been able to work from the Philippines, Thailand, and Vietnam. South East Asia is one of my favorite places to stay because of the weather, fascinating culture, low cost of living, and good food. Traveling makes me feel a sense of freedom that I don't get from an office.

To be honest, I don't even have to leave the USA to have a good time and feel free. Staycations are also nice. A staycation is where you just go to another city or state and hang out. I have hung out in Las Vegas, Aspen, Vail, Los Angeles, Miami, and other places. I do my regular hours of work, and then, after work, I go check out an art museum with my family, eat at amazing restaurants that are famous with the locals, or just go for a walk downtown.

Before COVID-19, it was harder to get a work from home position. But now, these remote positions are everywhere. During the lockdown, it became a necessity to have remote work capabilities.

As a result, it's now easier than ever to become a remote worker. Some companies have reported seeing an increase in productivity after allowing workers to work from home.

As of 2022, 10% of U.S. employees work from home. According to a study by Stanford Business, where they studied a travel agency with 16,000 employees, working from home saw a 13% increase in performance. Nine percent of this came from working more minutes per shift with fewer breaks and sick days, and 4% from more calls per minute. This increase may have come from a more comfortable and quiet working environment.

Working from home is a win-win scenario. The worker is in the best possible working environment to be more productive.

In this book, I'm going to tell you exactly how to find these remote positions.

Is WFH for you?

The terms WFH, work from home, remote work, telecommute and flex jobs are sometimes used interchangeably in organizations. What is different is how each organization defines them. We will go in greater detail about this, but we need to see if this is even something for you.

First, you should know that working from home is not for everyone. It sounds good, but, believe it or not, some people are not ready for it.

Here are some signs that it's not for you:

- You're an extrovert and absolutely love the feeling of being around many people
- You have small kids and will be disturbed all-day
- You live in a rural area with very poor Internet and electricity
- You struggle with self-discipline
- You don't have access to an Internet connection.
- You're not in an environment where you can work:
    - You don't have a quiet area
    - You don't have a room with privacy

If any of these apply to you and you cannot change the situation, you may want to reconsider the thought of working from home.

A good friend of mine tried doing 100% remote work, and she found out that she did not like it. She said she felt trapped in the house. When she worked remotely, she got depressed and restless.

She actually prefers to go into an office or visit sites to talk to customers and doesn't mind the commute.

I had multiple office coworkers tell me this. One told me he just didn't have the self-discipline to do it, and it was too tempting to sit around and play video games as much as possible. He said he gained a ton of weight and felt terrible. Another coworker told me that he did it for 15 years at IBM and preferred getting out of the house. The office was like a break for him. Remote work is just not for everyone.

Some of the challenges of working remotely

Self-discipline can be a challenge. Not everybody has the self-discipline to wake up in the morning, turn on the computer, and focus entirely on work, especially if there is a beach right outside, the kids want to go for a hike, or the dog wants you to throw the ball. I have to admit sometimes self-discipline is difficult.

Another bad thing about working from home is it sometimes I get close to my coworkers and would like to see them in person.

I've been doing this for many years now, and there are times when I just want to work in a different environment. On rare occasions, I have missed going to an office.

Another challenge of working from home is that sometimes, I get pulled into running errands around the house. These are things that do need to get done but could probably wait until after work.

You can't always do Staycations

I can't always travel when I am working from home. When I have a big project that requires me to lead a bunch of meetings, I am too busy to take the time to travel to a new destination, or I might have to work so many hours that it's not worth going anywhere, and I need to stay in the house.

I usually coordinate my trips so that I am not driving or flying while I am in the middle of my work from home jobs.

I had to do a vulnerability scan at a site, and on my way to the airport, my job kept trying to get a hold of me. Once I parked in long-term parking, I was able to respond to their emails. Every time I am on my way to a staycation spot to work from the Rocky Mountains or near the Las Vegas Strip, there is an emergency that forces me to stop everything I am doing and see what's going on. For this reason, I coordinate any travel time I have for the staycation so that I am en-route to the destination during non-work hours or take a day off unless I am on an actual business trip for my job.

Working after hours

Time management is another challenge you need to master. You would think the issue is working too little, but sometimes it's actually working too much.

One thing we take for granted when working in an office is that it physically separates our personal and work life. One challenge you may have is having the discipline to stop working.

One example from my own life is when I worked as a consultant on a big project and would get so wrapped up in getting it done that I would take calls when I was supposed to be off.

One time, I planned to head to another state with my son. We'd found a Samoyed puppy that we wanted, but the breeder was 700 miles away. Our plan was to head out on Friday right after work at 4:30 pm to Utah.

It had been a long week of reviewing a bunch of security controls for a client. I had already logged out of work when my work phone rang. It was the client.

I was already at a Shell station pumping gas and about to hit the road. I stared at the phone for a moment, debating on whether to answer the phone after business hours.

"Hello, Bruce Brown speaking. May I help you?"

The client had a complaint about the results of the last scan. They said it must have been a false positive because they were certain that they'd cleaned up the vulnerabilities that were showing up.

I assured them I would take a closer look, but the call lasted 10 miles away from the gas station. The client was in such a panic that I decided to call my boss and give him a heads-up. With all of the back and forth, that call cost me another hour of work.

If I had the self-discipline to manage my time, I would have disconnected from work at the end of the duty day.

The moral of the story is do not pick up the call from your job after hours.

The Time Zone Differences

I made it to the Philippines working a 6-figure job! I would be in South East Asia with close friends for a few weeks. We would travel to Thailand and Vietnam to hang out, drink, sightsee, and go to clubs.

But first, I had to finish a few days of work. It was easier said than done because I had to wake up at 10 pm and work until 7:30 am Philippines time. In Colorado, USA (mountain standard time), that was 7:00 am – 4:30 pm. It is a 15-hour time difference.

The hardest part was keeping up with meetings and calls. I had coworkers and clients on Central, Eastern, and Pacific time. Meanwhile, I was trying to keep track of the Philippines' time.

I would use Outlook or Google calendar on Mountain time to keep track. If my coworker said, "Let's have a call at 3 pm," I would make sure to put it on the calendar and send them a meeting invite to confirm the time.

I could not keep the times straight manually. Any attempt to calculate the time zone differences would result in me missing the meeting. So, I used online tools to keep up with time zones and days. I guess some people are very good at this, but I am really bad at keeping track of meetings in different time zones.

I can understand why a person would not want to work remotely. There may come a time when most jobs that can be done remotely will be. It's cheaper for organizations to allow it, making them more resilient against disasters and pandemics.

What You Need to have to Work From Home

Working from home is for people who are self-directed and have the self-discipline to work from anywhere. They can either silence the distractions or find a way to work through them.

- Are you great at managing your own time and don't need a supervisor or boss hovering over your cubicle?

- Are you just as good in meetings on a phone or video call as you are in person?
- Do you feel more comfortable doing work in your home office than in a cold, fluorescent yellow room where people gossip too loud by the water cooler?
- If you have a strong conviction that the time you just spent driving for 25 minutes could have been used to make a cup of coffee and run a vulnerability scan, then you should definitely join Team "Work From Home."

Things You Need Before You Work From Home for Cybersecurity

There are some basic things you will need:

- Stable electricity
- Internet with at least 3 to 12 Megabits per second (4G)
- A room with privacy and quiet
- A computer and a phone
- The right mindset

Electric

Electric power seems too obvious even to mention, but I wanted to talk about it because I have been to some parts of the world that had power spikes, brownouts, and blackouts. For example, when working from provincial parts of Thailand and the Philippines, I had to consider the lack of power. This mostly happens during the rainy season, when there are storms that take out the electricity for hours or even days.

In cybersecurity or any IT type job, I need more than just my phone to work. So, I would have to consider a workaround like a generator, power-saving configurations, additional chargers, or even staying in more expensive parts of the country that are not as impacted by storms.

Electricity is usually not a problem unless I am in a very provincial area of the world, and even then, with proper planning, I am able to keep working.

Internet

The best Internet setup for most work from home jobs is the following:

- Over 3 Megabits per second of stable Internet (download)
- At least 2 Megabits per second (upload)
- (2) separate Internet connections
- Security features enabled on your work laptop and phone
- Private and secure Internet connection
- Wired or Wireless with WPA 2 Encryption
- Access to a VPN (when in public areas)

These days, you can get the Internet just about anywhere because you can use your smartphone as a hotspot. With a decent old 4G connection that gives you a 3 – 12 Megabits per second connection, you can have an Internet connection that's good enough for most jobs.

For most jobs, not all jobs. Depending the amount of video conferencing, streaming, downloads and uploads, you may need way more bandwidth than 3 Megabits. Also, I have found a spotty 3 Megabit per second hotspot to be very problematic, particularly with cybersecurity analyst work where I needed to upload or download 1 Gigabit or larger files.

The rural parts of the USA are a great example where Internet access can be a huge issue. There are areas in Nevada, Colorado, Utah and Wyoming (for example) where it's like a baron wasteland, and there is no cell tower coverage for hundreds of miles. Areas like this would make it impossible to do remote work.

Another thing to consider is having two separate Internet connections. You could have one at home and one from your phone as a hotspot. Or even two phones that allow a hotspot connection. This is helpful because even the best Internet connections goes down from time to time. You want to have a second connection ready.

Security Features on your Computer

Protection of the data on the Internet is also important. With a cybersecurity job, a lot of the information you work with will be sensitive, private, or specialized information that could be damaging if it is made public. As much as possible, you will want to work from a private Internet with at least basic security features like a firewall and antivirus. If you happen to work in a public area, such as the library or Starbucks, you must be mindful of your surroundings and not work on sensitive information. You can use a VPN, a host-based firewall, and host-based intrusion protection, but none of this can guarantee that your system and the data you are working on won't be compromised. For cybersecurity work do not work from a public Internet connection.

If you do use wireless in public or even on your secure home network, you need to use WPA 2 as your encryption. Never use open networks, WEP, or WPA because they are not secure and can easily be hacked.

Storage encryption is another consideration. This will encrypt the data on the work system when it is not being used.

Many of these features will be implemented on a system or mobile device that is provided to you by the employer, but if they don't and you're using your own system, you need to have the following:

- Storage encryption
- Host-based security
- VPNs
- Secure wireless
- Never work from public wireless

You Need a Quiet, Secure Place

You need a place that's both quiet and private because many cybersecurity jobs require regular teleconference meetings where you discuss information or situations that are sensitive.

You may be talking about something within the organization that can hurt their reputation or allow an attacker leverage. For example, suppose you are looking at a bank's vulnerability scan report and you have a meeting with the chief information security officer about which items should be fixed first. In that case, you probably don't want to have members of that bank overhear you talking about it.

Sometimes, it's not just privacy but quiet that you need, just an hour or so of undisturbed silence to get through a meeting or focus on deep analysis of lots of data. This is very difficult to do if you have little kids and cannot lock the doors.

I started this many years ago when my kids were small. They could not understand that their dad had to work. They kept trying to play whenever they saw me.

If you have a separate room where you can separate yourself long enough to do the heavy work, then little kids, loud dogs, or even traffic outside is less of a problem.

Physical security is important to the data you work with. If you cannot secure your work computer or mobile device in a place where it cannot be stolen or tampered with, then working remotely will be a challenge. You need to know that the client's data cannot be accessed or manipulated by unauthorized people. If a person has possession of your work computer, then they can tamper with, corrupt, or steal the data with the right tools.

Other Equipment You May Need

Most of the organizations that had me working from home provided me with a laptop and sometimes a mobile phone. These devices were completely controlled and monitored by the organization. I've been given wireless scanners, thumb drives, and laptop accessories, including a docking station, smart card readers, and an ergonomic desk.

On a few occasions, I had to use my own equipment. I used my own computer and cell phone. These jobs typically did not have sensitive information.

Remote Work Restrictions

One of my favorite things is traveling while doing remote work. But some of the jobs I've worked for have restrictions based on the industry, country, or state laws. For example, as of this writing, the U.S. government has bans on trade with several countries. Some of them are:

- Cuba
- Iran
- Syria
- Venezuela
- China

If you work with the U.S. government handling sensitive information, highly technical equipment, intelligence, national security, or trade secrets, there will be conditions on your travel.

Depending on the job, you may not be allowed to take the organization's equipment outside of the country at all or even work outside of the state. Sometimes these conditions are simply notifying the organization you work for where you're going. You might get a briefing that gives you an idea of the threats in a particular part of the world.

Common travel tips and rules they give you are:

- Maintain physical protection of your government-furnished equipment (GFE) at all times.
- Be suspicious of strangers asking you questions about your job.

- Have situational awareness and always be aware of your surroundings.
- GFE can only be used in approved geographic locations and only for work purposes

The list of barred countries, restrictions, and tips changes from time to time. Before you travel, you will need to get with human resources to read the organization's travel restrictions.

The travel policy will give you a summary of what you can and cannot do without reading through actual federal laws and industry standards.

These policies come from regulations such as Arms Export Control Act (AECA), Export Administration Regulations (EAR), the International Traffic in Arms Regulations (ITAR), and the United States Munitions List (USML). These are United States regulations that restrict and control the export of defense and military-related technologies. This is to safeguard U.S. national security.

And if you're thinking, "Bruce, you're an American asshole! I don't even work for the U.S. government, and I never will! I don't need to think about this stuff at all."

First of all... "Rude."

Second, every country and industry has these types of rules depending on the classification of the information you work with. As a cybersecurity professional, you will have more exposure to sensitive information than in most other career fields.

These regulations include technical data, defense services, aircraft materials, and many other items. The regulations apply to manufacturers, exporters, distributors, 3rd party suppliers, contractors, and software and hardware providers for defense.

To comply with these regulations, organizations register with the State Department or equivalent and adopt an internal policy to enforce the laws. The penalties for violating these regulations are harsh, so they take them seriously.

A friend of mine had a job so sensitive that they (the government or the company or both) controlled and monitored his travel. His job directly affected national security. He had to carry his government phone everywhere he went. It was like a digital leash.

His classification was so high that I asked him if the U.S. government had any information on UFOs and aliens.

And he said...

He said something I would not write in a cybersecurity jobs book.

Most organizations do not have any ITAR restrictions. But if the organization has any affiliation or contract work with the government, there is a good chance that there are international restrictions.

Types of Work from home Cybersecurity Jobs

Many people want to work from home, but if you have never done it before, you should know that not all work from home jobs are equal.

Organizations will have a "remote work," "telecommute," or "work from home" policy where they have rules and restrictions on the remote work that they allow. This makes for a completely different work from home experience at each position.

I have been in different remote work situations, and, honestly, sometimes, it's better to work from the office. Not all remote work is good.

In my experience, you have different types of remote work jobs:

- Flex Work
- Remote with travel
- 100% Remote

Let's talk about each of these.

Flex Work

In cybersecurity, flex work schedules mean you will be expected to work from the office a few times per week. There is usually a reason why these jobs require people to work from the office. Sometimes they require at least weekly face-to-face meetings with the customer.

There are also situations where the data is too sensitive to bring home. In one IT job, I had that was flexible, we had a classified environment that could not be maintained remotely.

We had a lab with a network that had a "Secret" classification. The network had a firewall, routers, switches, and endpoint devices. It could not be accessed remotely. All work on this network was restricted to the lab.

When the commute time is too long, organizations will allow flex work from time to time. I worked at a place that preferred everyone to work from the office, but we were all in different states, so most of your work had to be remote. We had cybersecurity professionals near client sites, but sometimes their commute was over 2 hours, so the organization would allow them to go to the office only when absolutely necessary.

There are some organizations that have a strong culture of comradery and make it mandatory to meet in person a few times a week.

Federal organizations are starting to open up to a flexible work environment to attract more cybersecurity talent.

Remote Work With Travel

I had a job that was remote, but I traveled for over 50% of the year. I don't know if you could call it "work from home" because I was never home.

I was traveling to sites to teach security compliance. In January, I traveled to Japan and Germany. Then, in February, I would be in Virginia and Hawaii. I was at each site for 4 – 5 days teaching. This doesn't sound too bad, but you have to factor in the travel days. Depending on the distance between locations, there might be 2 – 3 days of travel, 4 days if something goes wrong with the flight. At times, I would be away from home for about two weeks out of the month. On the days I was home, I would be preparing for my next class. It felt like I was gone all the time.

Aside from different remote work situations, there are also just bad work environments. I am not going to say any names, but I worked for one organization that made our lives a living hell. They would have us deliver a 50-page document and then have us redo it. They would call us into meetings and berate us in front of our peers. The client would go directly to our boss for minor issues and tell them we were incompetent. They would attack us on emails addressed to our supervisors, their bosses, and our coworkers.

It was a terrible situation where there was a lot of stress. There was an internal investigation where the organization found out that parts of the leaders among our clients didn't like the contract, so they were trying to sabotage it. It was so bad that congress got involved. As I said, it was bad.

We had flex workers, office workers, and people who worked 100% remote, and we all had a very bad time at that organization. Not all work from home situations are good.

If you find yourself in an environment that is toxic, working from home will not help you. It's best to just seek other employment.

Find a "Work from Home" Cybersecurity Job

These days most search engines and job sites have filters, categories, and other features that allow you to find a work from home job. You don't need to go to a specialized remote work site, although some of those are good.

The best method I have found for getting offered more work from home opportunities is to market my resume specifically for these positions. Using the simple methods I will describe, I have been able to get more technical recruiters and jobs contacting me for remote positions than I have applied for.

I do this in three steps:

- Remote Work Resume
- Upload to Multiple Job Sites
- Apply to Work From Home Jobs

We will go into greater detail on each of these, but you must know that these jobs are more competitive than normal jobs. More qualified people will be applying for these work from home positions. As a result, these jobs take longer to get.

In my experience, a normal job might take me three weeks to get from the time I apply to the time I get the offer letter. Work from home jobs take me longer to get on average. This may be because I am very picky and looking for higher pay positions.

I have found I need to be way faster in applying for jobs, and I need to apply for way more work from home jobs than the regular ones.

When you approach the work from home resume, you will need to add more keywords to attract more employers and technical recruiters. You will need to post your resume in twice as many places.

Remote Work Resume

The first thing we will do is create a simple application tracking system (ATS) compliant resume. This resume needs keywords relevant to the cybersecurity position you are trying to get into.

To get a free sample of an ATS-style cybersecurity resume, go to:

convocourses.com/courses/resume

An ATS-style resume for cybersecurity looks like this:

Brian Noble

Phone number – email – City

Summary

Remote work preferred. 2 years of IT experience with a Public Trust security clearance. Skilled cybersecurity professional able to perform in a team and independently to get the jobs done. Well-versed in implementing NIST 800 and CIS-based security controls.

Education

Associate Degree – Information Technology – Fayetteville Community College – 2019

- Working on B.S. in C.S.
- Extensive training using digital spreadsheets and formulas efficiently
- Earned a certificate in Security+ training

Certifications

CompTIA Security + Certification

Project Management Professional Certification (PMP)

Work Experience

Help Desk Support – TirePlanet – remote – April 2021–April 2022

- Troubleshooting end-users' laptops with network and software issues; supporting 150 users with multiple devices
- Managed Android and iPhone ensuring all company-owned mobile devices are tracked and data is encrypted
- Enabled audit logs on 34 mission-essential systems and 100 end-user laptops to conduct continuous monitoring and detect possible security incidents
- Created an incident response plan for all business essential servers supporting the southwest sites; virtual servers include Windows 2019 and RedHat systems

IT Customer Service – Ants – New Mexico – January 2020–December 2021

- Conducted quarterly risk assessment on over 200 business critical systems; created risk reports for the CIO and upper management
- Assisted the server team in installing 12 Windows 2019 servers, migrating legacy systems to a new operating system
- Provided remote technical support for the workstations of over 1,500 customers; patient with difficult customers

Skills

- Programming language: C+, HTML, Fortran, COBOL
- Security clearance: Secret, TS/SCI, Public Trust

The template is the easy part. What will take some work on your part is to get keywords into the resume. To find the correct keywords, you will need to research the market for the job you want.

For example, if you are trying to go into "cybersecurity investigations" or "cybersecurity analyst" work, you will need to start by conducting a search on that key phrase.

Use job sites and aggregators to search your key phrase of choice. You are looking for employers that have recently put out jobs for that key phrase.

Pay close attention to the job description requirements, skills, certifications, tools, and other things employers are looking for.

On LinkedIn, you can take this search deeper by looking into other people's resumes. Look for cybersecurity professionals in your field of choice and check out what keywords they have chosen.

You will want to use the same keywords, tools, and skills on your resume. I am not telling you to lie on your resume; I am telling you to look at your own skills, experience, and knowledge and use the same wording that the cybersecurity market is looking for.

For more on keywords and resume marketing, check out book 1, *Cybersecurity jobs Resume Marketing,* or check out the course at convocourses.com

In this book, our main focus will be targeting cybersecurity work from home positions.

Work From Home Summary

For remote work in cybersecurity, we need to use the magic words: "Remote Work"

Well, actually, you have a few other magic words:

"Work from home"

"Hybrid"

"Telecommute"

You want to put this in your resume. In fact, you want to put them in the summary of your resume like this:

Summary

Work from home preferred. 3 years of cybersecurity, implementing security controls on business essential functions in accordance with security best practices detailed in CIS v8.

This summary has some keywords and starts off with our desire to "work from home." This is important because some technical recruiters and employers look for this.

I usually use the words "remote work preferred," but "work from home," "hybrid," and "telecommute" are more popular.

Experience Working Remotely

In 50% of the interviews I've had for "work from home" positions, they asked me if I have worked from home before. They ask this because not everyone does well in a work from home environment.

One of the first things you can do to indicate that you have worked remotely is to put it on top of your work experience, where you normally put the location of your previous employment. It will read like this:

IT Specialist

Oracle Labs, Remote; February 2020 to Current

Normally, the location of the business is put right up top just before the time frame that you worked there, but this is an opportunity to show that you worked remotely.

After listing the role, location, and timeframe, you can also mention that you worked from home like this:

- Updated security patches on 150 endpoint devices working from home, reducing the overall risks to the organization
- Wrote 4 enterprise-level cybersecurity policies and standards for a fortune 500 company coordinating with upper-level management while working from home

If you have never actually "worked from home," you have more than likely done lots of work remotely. Most organizations have systems that are at remote locations, and you can use this on your resume. If you have had any of the following situations, you have had exposure to remote work or remote work tools:

- Did the organization you work for allow VPNs?
- Did the employer allow flex work allowing people to work from home a few times a week?
- Did the business have sites at different locations?
- Did you ever have to do meetings over the phone?
- Were audio or video group calls ever done at the place you worked?
- Did you ever have to use Zoom, Teams, Skype, Webex, or any other video conferencing tools to coordinate with others to get work done?
- Did you have calls with clients and customers to help them with a technical service?

If you have worked in any of these situations, there may be something you can put on your resume about working remotely or working with tools for working remotely. Let me explain how you can mention this in your work experience.

- Serviced 164 endpoint devices for remote work employees by updating security patches and antivirus signatures on them; improved the resilience of the organization's business function

- Subject matter expert on regular remote configuration management meetings that included major Windows Server 2019 migration; meetings completed via Zoom and Teams collaborations

In these two examples, we managed to squeeze in the keyword "remote." We also explain that we have been successful in doing remote work. In the example, we mention the latest and greatest video conferencing tools.

While we can work well in a team collaborating remotely, we want to mention that we can work independently with little or no instruction.

- Self-directed on large and small cybersecurity projects, such as the configuration of VPN on 67 mobile devices
- Initiated risk reduction tasks, including the creation of cybersecurity reports on the top 20 vulnerabilities within the organization

Employers want to know that you can work independently with no one constantly holding your hand. If you land a work from home job, you will need to be able to get the job done with little or no supervision. So we want to put this in the resume.

You will also notice that I use numbers in the sample resume text. This is done to show the impact of cybersecurity actions.

To get a free sample of an ATS-style cybersecurity resume, go to:

convocourses.com/courses/resume

Market Your WFH Resume

Once you have a solid resume stating your preference for a work from home job and your ability to work remotely, it's time to publish this resume on the job sites.

Find the Top 10 Job Sites

Search for the top job sites in your country. You can do this by going to your favorite search engine and typing the key phrase:

- Top Job Sites in the USA
- Top Job Sites in Canada
- Top Job Sites in the U.K.
- Top Job Sites in Kenya

Use whatever country you are trying to get work in. Since this is a work from home job, it can be any country. But just know that each country has its own challenges, laws, and restrictions.

Some countries don't have many remote jobs because they don't have the infrastructure or culture to allow work from home. Sometimes "work from home" is just not a thing there.

Many cybersecurity jobs in the USA restrict foreign nationals from working with sensitive data. There are jobs that hire foreign nationals, but you just have to look for them.

Some companies allow remote work, but only if you work remotely from their country.

Finding work from home jobs that will fit your situation is going to be hard, so you will need to find at least ten of the top job sites to post your resume.

If you are really serious, find 20 or 30 sites in more than one country.

Create a Profile Post Your Resume

WARNING:

We interrupt this book for a warning about how effective this is! *This really works! Once I did this, I started getting contacted by dozens of technical recruiters and employers per week. I strongly suggest you use a throw-away email and a different phone number. This is so effective that I get contacts throughout the day at inconvenient times.*

You must use a different email, not post your full address, and must use a different phone number. This is not a joke.

This part of the process will take the longest time, especially if you are posting on ten sites. A solid ATS-style resume will make your work here easier because many sites just allow you to upload your resume, and 50% of the work is done.

The most effective job sites will have a detailed profile for you to fill out. You will need to take time to properly complete this because the site will use this profile to find you. The site's algorithm will use the data in the profile and your uploaded resume to match you with jobs.

So, when the profile has a section to fill out your skills, you must put in all your cybersecurity skills. For a deeper dive into some suggested career paths and associated skills, check out *Book 2: Cybersecurity Jobs and Career Paths.* You can also use other people's resumes posted on sites like LinkedIn.

The only parts of the profile you will skip are the ones that are not relevant.

For example, I don't know any other languages, so I have to skip the language section. But if you know more than one language, that's a big deal, and you need to put that on your profile.

The profile is very important for work from home cybersecurity jobs because most employers and technical recruiters are looking at the top 10 job sites. If your profile doesn't list a valuable skill, certification, or experience that they are looking for, they will find someone else. And if you don't even have a profile, they will not find you at all.

The more time you put into filling out these profiles, the better your chances because it will increase your probability of being found.

For a deeper dive into resume marketing, check out *Book 1: Cybersecurity Jobs Resume Marketing*.

Apply for Remote Jobs

To get a good work from home job, it's not enough to have a good resume and post it on ten job sites. The next step is also important. You need to apply for as many remote jobs as possible.

Once your perfect, ATS-style cybersecurity resume is posted on NO less than ten of the top job sites, you need to conduct a search for jobs on that site.

The great thing about posting on these job sites and filling out a complete profile is that the site will do most of the work for you. As I said, the algorithm will actively find jobs that match you.

But with work from home jobs, there is one more step we need to take to find these jobs.

We need to filter for remote positions. For example, if we're looking for an "IT customer support" job, we want to filter for "remote work."

Cybersecurity Jobs: Work From Home

Most of the top job sites have a filter called "remote work" or "work from home."

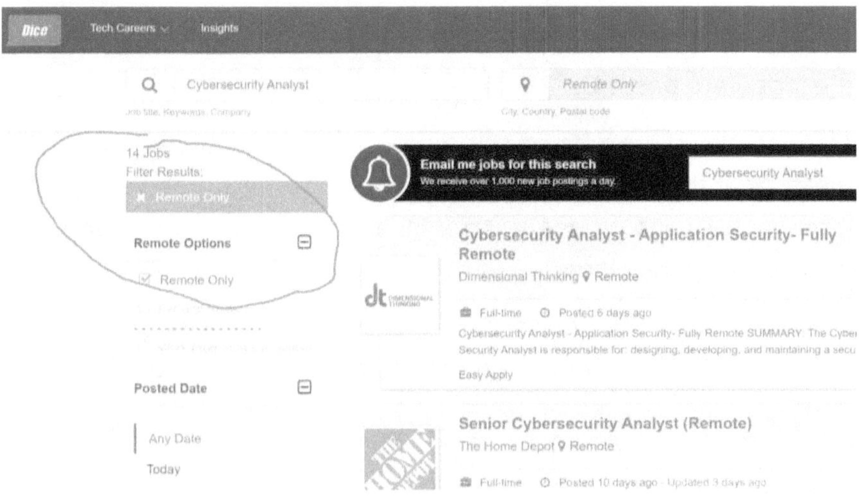

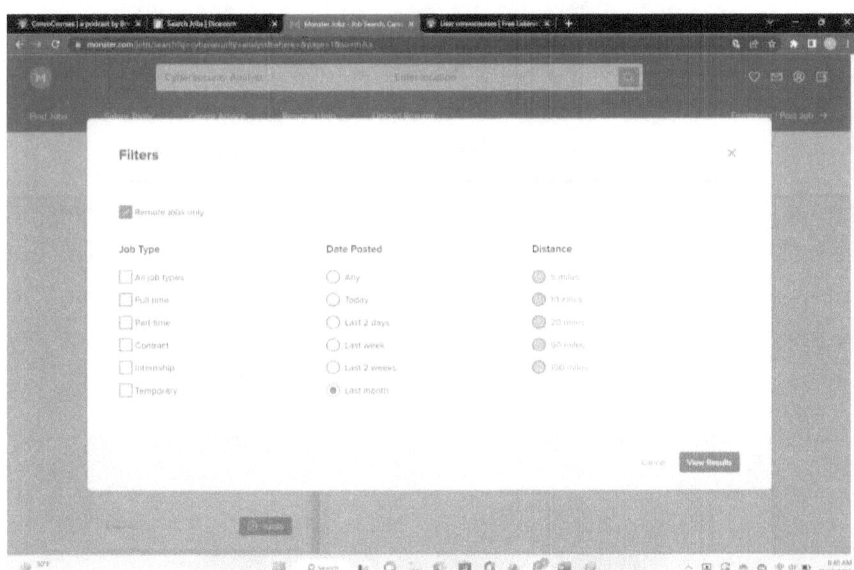

For example, the job search site Dice.com has a "Remote Only" check box. Monster.com and others also have this feature.

Another thing you want to add to the filter is a time frame of when the jobs were posted.

The default time frame of posting on some job sites is "Any." This means that the search results come from positions that were posted three months ago or longer. After 30 days, work from home jobs are usually long gone (especially if they are good or pay well).

You need to use this filter and look for jobs that have been posted in the last 30 days or sooner; work from home jobs are taken fast.

Remote work is much more competitive than the regular local jobs out there. You will need to apply for as many remote, flex, telecommute, and 100% work from home jobs as possible.

We want to do this on multiple sites. I cannot stress this enough. Three of four top sites will not be enough to get a remote job. You need to apply for dozens of jobs on ten or more job sites.

The search engines, Google.com, Bing, and others also have job search features. They are usually just pulling data from all over the Internet to show you results, but all you have to do is type in "Cybersecurity Jobs." Really, anything searched with "Jobs" in the key phrase will have the search engines job aggregator pop up.

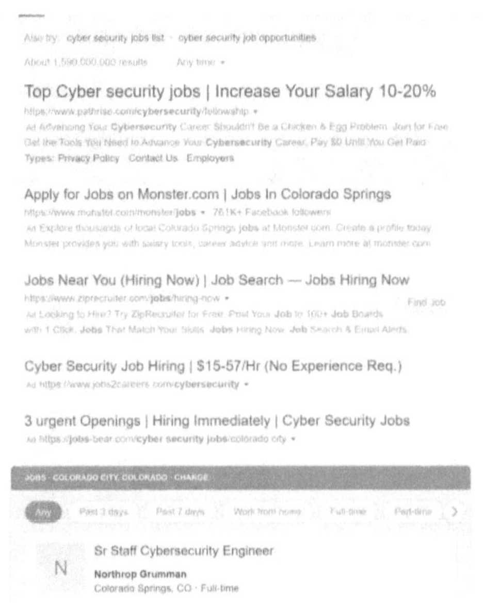
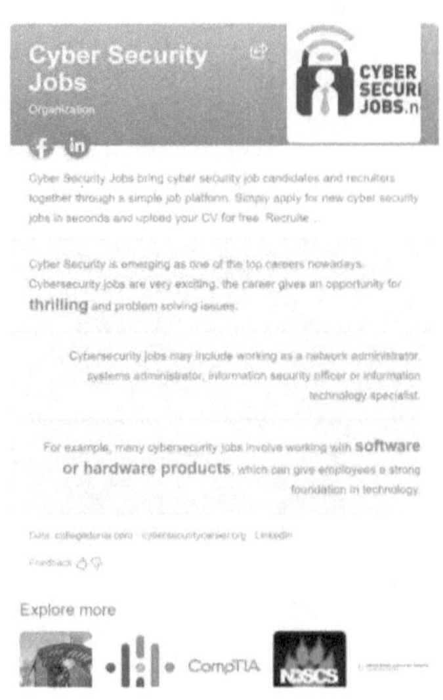

Use Alerts & Notifications

Most job sites have a feature that will notify you when a job matches what you are looking for. As soon as the employer posts the job, the site will send you a text or email. This feature is called "Alerts" or "Notifications."

With work from home jobs, this is something you may want to use because these jobs go very fast.

How you set up the alert depends on the job site aggregator. With Google jobs, Linkedin, and Dice.com, you conduct a search for the cybersecurity job you are looking for. So you would do your normal job search, such as "cybersecurity analyst." If you are having a hard time finding a position, make sure it is a broad term such as "cybersecurity" filter for "remote work only," and you can set up the alert after the search.

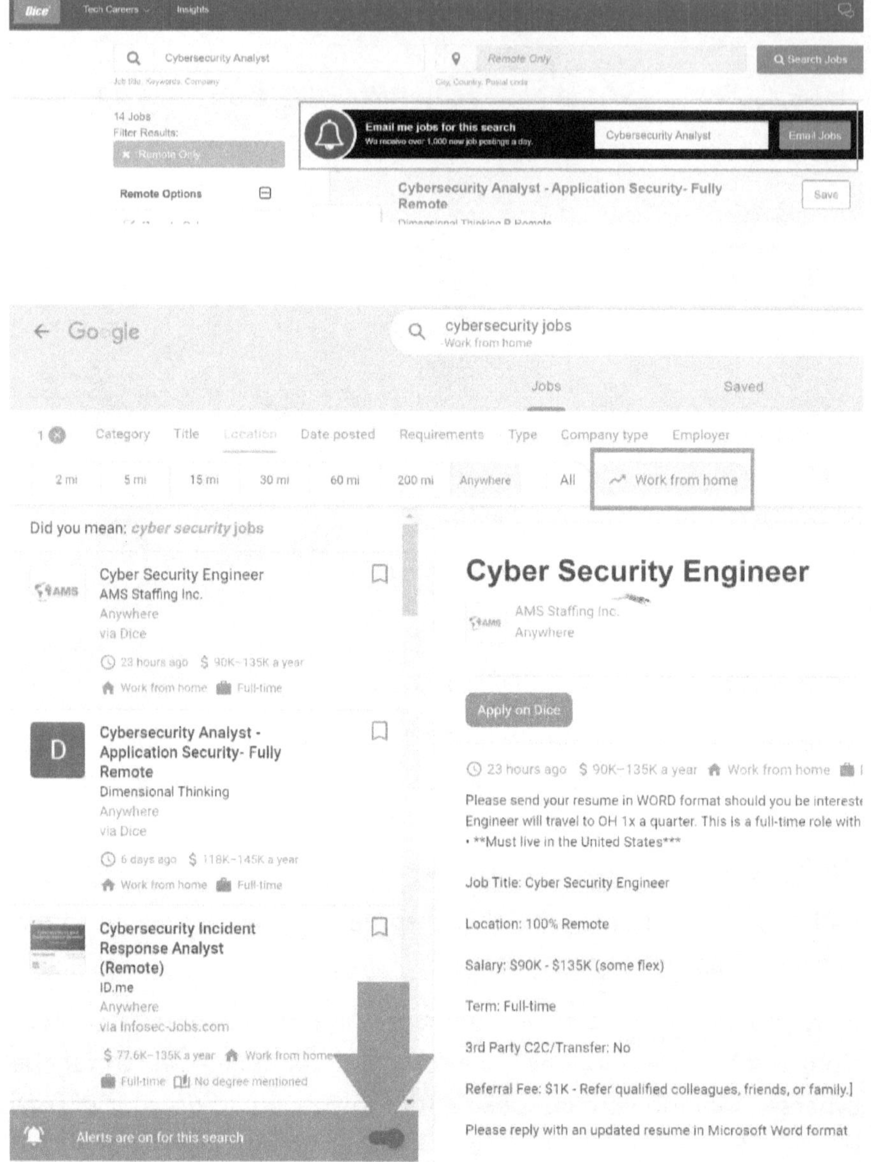
Dice
Tech Careers
Insights
Cybersecurity Analyst
Job Title, Keywords, Company
Remote Only
City, Country, Postal code
Search Jobs
14 Jobs
Filter Results:
Remote Only
Email me jobs for this search
We receive over 1,000 new job postings a day.
Cybersecurity Analyst
Email Jobs
Remote Options
Cybersecurity Analyst - Application Security- Fully Remote
Dimensional Thinking R Remote
Save
Google
cybersecurity jobs
Work from home
Jobs
Saved
Category   Title   Location   Date posted   Requirements   Type   Company type   Employer
2 mi   5 mi   15 mi   30 mi   60 mi   200 mi   Anywhere   All   Work from home
Did you mean: cyber security jobs
Cyber Security Engineer
AMS Staffing Inc.
Anywhere
via Dice
23 hours ago $ 90K-135K a year
Work from home   Full-time
Cybersecurity Analyst - Application Security- Fully Remote
Dimensional Thinking
Anywhere
via Dice
6 days ago $ 118K-145K a year
Work from home   Full-time
Cybersecurity Incident Response Analyst (Remote)
ID.me
Anywhere
via Infosec-Jobs.com
$ 77.6K-135K a year   Work from home
Full-time   No degree mentioned
Alerts are on for this search
Cyber Security Engineer
AMS Staffing Inc.
Anywhere
Apply on Dice
23 hours ago $ 90K-135K a year   Work from home
Please send your resume in WORD format should you be intereste
Engineer will travel to OH 1x a quarter. This is a full-time role with
• **Must live in the United States***
Job Title: Cyber Security Engineer
Location: 100% Remote
Salary: $90K - $135K (some flex)
Term: Full-time
3rd Party C2C/Transfer: No
Referral Fee: $1K - Refer qualified colleagues, friends, or family.]
Please reply with an updated resume in Microsoft Word format

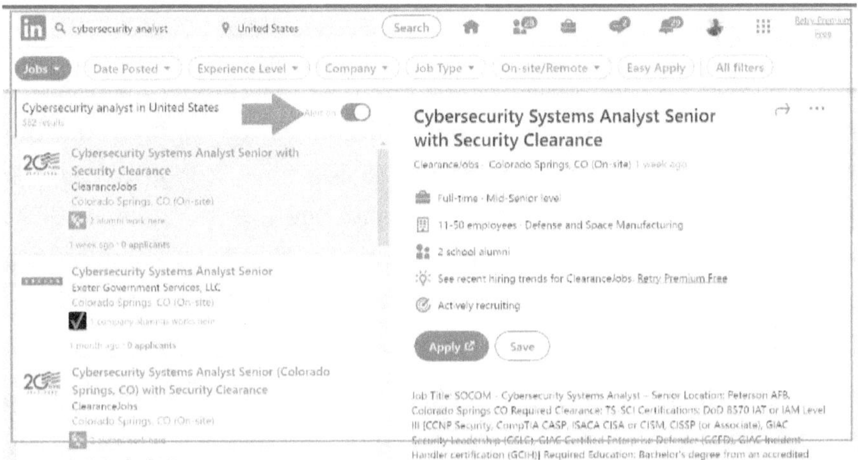

On Monster, the search is set up in a separate part of the site. Just be aware that you may need to hunt for this feature.

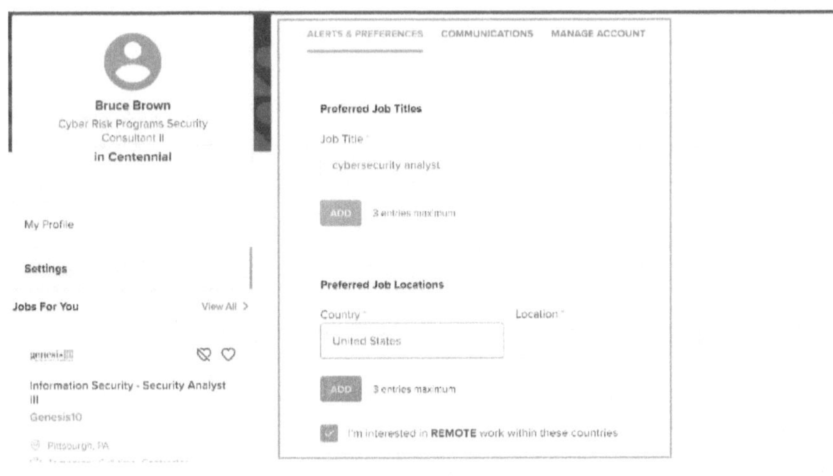

Be Open Minded

What I have had to do in finding remote positions is be open to different roles. There was a time when I ONLY wanted remote security information event manager (SIEM) jobs. It was because a former coworker told me that he had been working as a SIEM engineer from home, making about 200k. Another friend of mine was a Unix administrator working from home. These were both hands-on technical jobs.

I thought these were the only jobs available for remote work. I thought it had to be highly technical and from a very large company because anyone I knew who landed these rare remote jobs had this exact situation. I wanted this so bad that I got fixated on this one thing.

I was wrong.

I have had cybersecurity teaching jobs, policy writing jobs, and information system security jobs that were remote. I have been offered opportunities to do program management, system engineering, and a huge variety of jobs that were 100% remote.

You need to have an open mind for remote work because there are all kinds of situations and positions that need your help.

My first work from home position came from a blog post I did. I was writing a blog that broke down how to do security compliance for the government, and an employer found it.

She had a small business that had a 400,000-dollar contract with the military. She had so much work that she could no longer do it all herself. She reached out to me and offered me a job helping her teach.

That was also the first time I grossed 100,000 dollars for the year.

Avoid Scams

You have to be open minded, but you have to avoid scams.

In your search for remote jobs, you will definitely run into scams. I just want to warn you about this. There are a lot of scammers online offering remote positions. These people are trying to get you to give them your personally identifiable information and money or trying to exploit you in some way for their own gain.

Here are signs that let you know that you are probably dealing with a scam:

- If it sounds too good to be true, then it probably is
- If they are asking for personal information such as your social security number
- They want you to send them money before you have access to the employer
- The job has nothing to do with your profession
- They are offering a once-in-a-lifetime business opportunity
- They want you to download something or click a link before you can even have a screening interview.

I don't want to scare you from a great potential remote cybersecurity job. I just want you to proceed with caution and take time to research the potential employer.

There are some amazing opportunities that I have been offered. More than once, the owner of a small company called me, gave me a 20-minute Interview, and offered me a position immediately. It turned out to be real. They didn't ask me for my social or ask me to pay some fee before I got the job. In each case, the small business ended up giving me information that put them at risk because if I knew about the client and the contract, I could potentially solicit their customer directly. I knew it was real because I was able to verify the organization myself with the information they gave me about the work.

My point is whenever this happens, I am very suspicious! And you should be too. Don't jump into anything too fast. Remember, you are interviewing the employer as much as they are interviewing you. You need to do your due diligence. You need to research the organization. Check them out online. What is their reputation? Can you find others who have worked for them? Can you verify their real contact information? Are they putting themselves at risk just by telling you about the opportunity? For example, after a non-disclosure agreement, are they giving you sensitive information that could put their business at risk?

Work from home interview

With work from home jobs, it all comes down to the interview. This is sometimes the first and last time they will see your face, so you have to make it count.

More than normal office jobs, an online interview is pivotal for remote work. The resume just gets your foot in the door.

One of the things that you have to absolutely make sure is good is your internet connection and your online presentation:

- Your audio and visual during the interview has to be solid
- Make sure you are dressed in business casual
- Be online and ready before the interview starts

The interview process for cybersecurity usually consists of an average of three separate contacts before an actual job is offered. In my many interviews this process usually consists of the following:

- The screener contact
- Hiring manager/H.R. department Interview
- Manager/Technical Interview

The Screener

With cybersecurity jobs, you will usually have a screener contact you. This is a technical recruiter consisting of a call, an email, or both. They don't usually know much about IT or the actual job you will do. You are probably the fifty-seventh person they have emailed, called, or messaged for this position. This call will be short. They only want to know if you are interested in the position, if you are qualified, and if you are available. Sometimes, they will have you do a non-disclosure agreement if it is a staffing agency; this is a common practice. You don't need to give them any personal information at this point. There is no commitment to anything yet. I don't normally sign an NDA until I am sure I am qualified and want to know more about the opportunity. If I am interested, I start by reading the job description and requirements.

They may ask if you are willing to travel. Sometimes they will let you know about the salary range. If you match the job requirements and are interested, the screener will contact someone closer to the project. This will be the human resources department, a hiring manager, or even someone from the team you would be working with.

Hiring Manager and H.R. Department

If the organization's process is thorough, the screener will send your contact information and resume to an office that will conduct further screening. This will be the employer's hiring manager or Human Resources department. In my experience, this is a stress-free 15 to 20-minute introduction to the company over the phone.

They take a quick look at your resume. They ask more questions to see if you fit into the role. It is usually just an informal, informative session where they tell you about the company and the role that they are filling. Questions they ask include things like:

- Have you worked remotely before?
- Where are you currently working?
- Have you ever heard of our company before?
- Are you willing to travel (if applicable)?
- Are you willing to relocate (if applicable)?

They might ask very generic questions about your experience working with a certain aspect of cybersecurity or using a certain tool. For example, they might say something like:

"Can you tell me about your cybersecurity experience?"

Or

"Have you ever worked with the Department of Defense before?"

They explain the benefits, mention the salary, the hiring process, and other general information about working with the client and the company. At this point, they try to sell you on the idea of working for the company if they think you might be a good fit. There are no details about the tasks of the job because H.R. will not know much about it. Any questions you have will have to be about your work as an employee working for this employer.

On some occasions, the hiring managers tried to talk me into working locally or even relocating. Sometimes, it's just not a good fit, and we politely end the Interviewing process.

But if everything is good, the hiring manager or human resources office will set you up on a meeting with the technical team or the managers directly involved with the job. When this happens, I get a formal email inviting me to a video conference call.

Technical and Management Interview

In my last few interviews for remote jobs, the employer used the top enterprise-level video conferencing software. At the time of this writing, it has been Microsoft Teams, Zoom, Skype, or Webex.

Make sure you test the video conferencing software to make sure it works before the call.

You will be expected to turn on your video. What I do is download the applicable software and test the video and audio on the system I will be using. You may need to create an account on the application they are using.

I ensure the lighting is good and I am in a quiet room. If possible, record yourself with the software and watch yourself perform a mock interview.

Before the video, do the following:

- Review the job description and see how it matches your own experience
- Review your own resume
- Check the sound, lighting, and video using the software they selected
- Practice a mock interview
- Dress business casual
- Remove all background distractions

What you don't want to do is:

- Set everything up 5 minutes before the interview
- Have technical difficulties 10 minutes into the call
- Be smoking or eating chips during the interview
- Chewing gum during the interview
- Pretend like you know everything
- Wear pajamas with kids running around in the background

Instead, be on the call ready to go 15 minutes before the call. I have found 15 minutes is best because there are often technical difficulties that take a few minutes to fix. You need to be the best-dressed person on the call. While everybody else is dressed in their T-shirts and baseball caps, you will be in button-down business casual with the best mic and camera and be the most prepared person on the call.

If you take the time to dive deep into their job description and what they require, you will have a solid understanding of what kinds of questions they will ask.

During the interview, they will say things like:

> "I can see on your resume that you have experience setting up audit logs on Linux. Can you tell me more about that?"

> OR

> "The team really needs someone who knows how to implement patches on Windows and do vulnerability management. Do you have experience doing that?"

Open-ended questions are an opportunity to tell them about your experience. You need to look directly into the camera and answer just like you practiced.

There's a habit that we have of looking at ourselves when talking on video. We look at ourselves on the video screen while speaking, but when we do this, our eyes are not looking at the people we are talking to. You need to look into the lens of the camera and speak toward the mic. Practice doing this, record yourself doing it, and play it back.

The types of questions will be based on the requirements in the job description.

At the end of the interview, they will ask you if you have any questions for them. I usually ask questions to identify any red flags like overworked employees and travel. Here are some examples of questions that I ask:

- Is there any shift work?
- What are the typical work hours?
- Is there overtime?
- Who is the client?
- How much travel is there?
- Is there a high turnover rate?
- What are the biggest challenges of the position?
- How many systems will I manage?
- What are some pros and cons about the job?
- How much time off do we get per year?

Company Research

As much as they are interviewing you, you need to interview them. Look into what the company does, its objectives, its core values, and who they serve. You need to look into the following:

- How many sites do they have, and where are they located?
- Look at all the sites that they have all around the world.
- What is the organization's gross revenue?
- What are the salaries of average employees?
- Are employees posting negative comments are videos about them?
- Have they recently had a breach?

You might be able to find the average salary or even the position you are going for on sites like Payscale, Salary.com, or Glassdoor.

Go to social media to see if you can find former employees talking about the company.

You need to know exactly what you are getting into with the company.

One thing I want to repeat is to read through the job description, requirements, and preferences. Preferences will sometimes tell you a lot about what tools they use.

Two Remote Jobs

With remote work, I have had the opportunity to work two high-paying jobs at once. When you are not in an office, commuting to an office, or having coworkers chat you up about things that have little or nothing to do with your job, it's amazing how much extra time you have between creating reports, vulnerabilities to analyze, or meaningless impromptu meetings on the plan of action and milestones.

If you are considering doing this, make sure you don't have a conflict of interest with soulless litigious powerhouses like governments or financial institutions. For example, you should not work for two competing organizations in the same industry. Another example is working as an auditor and working for the organization that will be audited.

These types of shenanigans can win you a free lunch in federal prison or, at the very least, get you paying for a lawyer's hair transplant surgery. Hair transplants are not cheap, buddy. Trust me... I know.

Another thing to avoid is violating your contract. Some contracts explicitly tell you not to work for other organizations during work hours.

You might be thinking, "Bruce, I've been doing this for a while. I have not been caught."

Ok. If you want to be picking up soap in jail, be my guest. Listen, it's not illegal to do this (if you do it right). I am just saying to proceed with caution and at your own risk.

In cybersecurity, you will be offered many positions that you can do remotely, and it occurs to you that you can do more than one.

I have done it a few times. There is a right way and a wrong way to have two jobs.

I have done the following:

- Quick Temporary Side Jobs
- Secondary Part-time Cybersecurity Job
- Two Full-time jobs

Quick temporary side jobs

What I do from time to time is temporary cybersecurity work that consists of doing one task that will only take a few weeks or less to do. For example, it might be creating a system security plan or running a scan. This type of work is not dependent on my working in a shift or from 8 am to 4 pm because the focus is just to get the work done in a certain period. We just agree on what the work will be, how long it will take, and how much it will cost. This is usually an hourly rate, but I have written documents or created training for an organization for a flat fee.

These types of jobs are usually very small businesses that don't need anyone to do the work full-time because it is a one-time thing.

Secondary Part-time Cybersecurity Job

This is work where they don't need someone working 8 hours every day. But they need someone to fill a role with multiple tasks, talk to the clients, and join meetings.

This is doable, but I have had success with this only if I tell that part-time job that I have a full-time job. I have to let them know that my full-time job takes priority. This is important because there are occasions when your full-time position will overlap with the part-time job and you have to make sure this does not happen.

Two Full-Time Jobs

DO NOT DO THIS!

There are only 24 hours in a day. If you are working 16 hours a day, at weekends, and on holidays, you will burn out fast.

Psychologically, you will start to question the meaning of life. You start to think to yourself, "Am I only alive to work? How much money do I need?"

You will begin to have hallucinations, and you will go bald as you slowly descend into madness!

Ok, I am exaggerating, but I am telling you this is just not healthy. If you do decide to work two full-time jobs like an idiot, make sure you only do it for a limited amount of time because the stress of doing this in a cybersecurity position is very high.

It's your life, and you can do whatever you want. But if you have landed a really good full-time, cybersecurity position, 100% remote job with good pay and good benefits, take time to realize the risk you run by violating that organization's trust.

I have done it before, and I do not recommend it. Beyond risking the "trust of a company," it gets into working yourself to burn out. It's not fun.

Doing this pays like crazy. But remember this:

- Pigs get fat. Hogs get slaughtered.

You Can Do it

45

The last thing I want to say about getting a work from home job is that you can do it. There's a gold rush for these work from home positions in cybersecurity. As soon as they're posted, the best and brightest are going after these jobs. Competition is much more fierce with work from home positions.

Don't be discouraged. If you use the techniques in this book, you will get lots of opportunities for remote work.